Don't Shoot the Horse

§

BY
H. Randy Hayes

Copyright © 2007 by H. Randy Hayes

Don't Shoot the Horse
by H. Randy Hayes

Printed in the United States of America

ISBN 978-1-60266-907-9

All rights reserved solely by the author. The author guarantees all contents are original and do not infringe upon the legal rights of any other person or work. No part of this book may be reproduced in any form without the permission of the author. The views expressed in this book are not necessarily those of the publisher.

Unless otherwise indicated, Bible quotations are taken from:

The King James version of the Bible.

The Living Bible. Copyright © 1971 by Tyndale House Publishers, Wheaton, IL.

The Revised Standard Version of the Bible. Copyright © 1946, 1952, 1971 by Division of Christian Education of the National Council of Churches of Christ in the USA.

www.xulonpress.com

Acknowledgments:

There are a lot of people that helped to make this work possible. I would like to give my heart felt thanks for their encouragement and support. First there are my parents who believed in me and opened their home and their hearts when I needed them the most. I would like to thank my girls, Erica, my daughter, and Kellie, my niece, for their support and comfort when I needed them the most. I would like to thank all the friends that stood behind me and encouraged me through some very hard times. I would like to give a very special thanks to my sister, Lori, and friend, Heidi, who also gave support and encouragement, and proof read this book, I would also like to thank them for keeping quite how many mistakes they had to correct.
Thank you, I love you all.

H. Randy Hayes

Chapters

Don't shoot the horse 9
Yelling into the refrigerator 17
When words fall short 23
What happened to the fish? 27
It Should not Happen this way 33
Christ like in short shorts 41
Beyond the shadow of a cloud 45
Raped by bitterness 51
Behind a slow driver 65
We all have shoes 71
Why a Manger 75
Stories told to me 83
Regaining your wow 87
Resurrection of the Heart 93
Mysteries and secrets 111
Thanks a lot 123
The God of Broken Pieces 133
Regaining your footing 145
Under the influence 155
Regaining your Smile 167
The Bethesda Syndrome 179
The End 185

Chapter 1

Don't shoot the horse

At one time, not so long ago, farmers, ranchers, and anyone else who owned horses would "put them out of their misery" when the horse broke a leg. Shooting them was done as an act of mercy. The problem I have with this solution is that it was no solution at all. Instead of having a horse with a broken leg, you would have a dead horse with a broken leg. The problem of the broken leg was never addressed. Today many horses are still shot because of economic reasons, it is simply cheaper to "put the horse down" and buy a new one, rather than expend the time and finances required to rehabilitate it. Therefore, it simply comes down to how valuable something is to us. The horse trainer that I spoke to told me that it might take up to two years before the horse would be able to run again. Are two years to long to wait for something that is valuable to you?

A family should be a valuable thing to us, but how many marriages are broken up because of problems that would take to long to solve? It is kind of like shooting the horse. Maybe it would take two years for that wife to really forgive the foolishness of her husband. It might take that long for a husband to get over a deep hurt. Therefore, the question would be "how valuable is the marriage?" In addition, if the problems are not solved do we carry that unforgiveness and hurt into the second marriage? I think so.

We face many problems today that would be better solved than "bailed out of". People "bail out" of their churches, their jobs, communities, families and many difficult stages in their lives rather than face them. Problems are solvable, circumstances are survivable, and situations can be overcome, if people would be a little more committed to seeing things through.

Sometimes problems are not as big as they appear, and not as impossible as they project themselves to be. Once I thought I had discovered something wrong with me, using a book about the human body, I diagnosed myself as having a tumor. I worried over this until I got an appointment with the Doctor. The Doctor sent me for X-rays and told me to come back in a few days. The morning that I was to go to the Doctor, the hospital called and asked me to come back for more X-rays. The fear of what might be, made the problem look like a giant to me. I had the X-rays made and went over to the Doctor's office for the news. By the time they called my name I had almost made myself sick with concern. The nurse led me to a little room with a little metal stool and then LIED when she said, "the Doctor will be right with you". I always thought that "right with you" meant that he was on his way. The longer I waited the bigger my problem got, it felt like something was clawing my insides out. I remembered that verse in 2nd Timothy that says, *"For God hath not given us the spirit of fear; but of power, and of love, and of a sound mind."* So I sat in that little room, prayed, and rebuked the spirit of fear, suddenly the fear just drained out of me.

Spirit or not, I will leave that to the theologians to debate, all I know is that day I faced the fear and overcame. When the Doctor FINALLY made it to my closet, he let me know that there was nothing wrong with me (physically). The problems looked and felt a lot bigger than they were.

The story of David and Goliath is a good example; it is amazing that Israel's smallest was greater than the Philistines' biggest. You find the story in First Samuel, Seventeen.

> *4. And there went out a champion out of the camp of the Philistines, named Goliath, of Gath, whose height was six cubits and a span.*

Do you think that the devil might have champions that come against us? I do. The Bible tells us that Satan is out there to steal, kill and destroy us. How does he do this? He sends out champions against us, giants that bring fear, confusion and many times hopelessness. Who are these champions of the devil? Cancer would be one, or any illness that would hinder your faith. Divorce would be another. Hurt and disappointment in the church would be among them. Since Jesus came that we would have life more abundantly anything that would hinder that, I would classify as a champion of the devil. Did you notice how big this giant was? Goliath was over nine feet tall; no one in his right mind would want to go up against something that big. Do you think that the devil will try his best to make his champions look as big as possible? I do. It is not how big your adversary is that matters; it is how big the one standing with you is. David may have been smaller than Goliath but God was bigger than Goliath and the entire Philistine army. God is also bigger than addiction to drugs, alcohol or pornography; He is bigger than any disease or situation you can think of. Philippians 2:9 tells us that the name of Jesus is above every name. Everything that has a name, cancer, stress, emotional turmoil or any circumstance we may find ourselves in, comes under the name of Jesus. The name of Jesus is bigger than all the giants that come against us.

5. And he had an helmet of brass upon his head, and he was armed with a coat of mail; and the weight of the coat was five thousand shekels of brass.

6. And he had greaves of brass upon his legs, and a target of brass between his shoulders.

This person looks invincible, there is no way that a man could penetrate that armor, but there is a God who not only knows all the enemies weaknesses, but all the enemies' strengths are weak to Him. Do not fret over the impossibilities of the things you face, but the possibilities that lie in the creator of this universe

Verse 26. for who is this uncircumcised Philistine, that he should defy the armies of the living God?

I love David's attitude here, "who is he to challenge GOD"!!!! I have a daughter and anyone who comes against her has me to deal with, I do not even like it when the umpire call a strike on her. We are the children of God and anyone or thing that comes against us has God to deal with. We just need to learn to let God handle things, and most of the time without our help.

Verse 33. And Saul said to David, Thou art not able to go against this Philistine to fight with him: for thou art but a youth, and he a man of war from his youth.

When you face your giants there will be friends like Job had to "encourage" you and let you know what is impossible and not. Remember that the miracles God works in our lives are only miracles to us, to God they are only spoken words. Do what David did, remember your past victories.

34. And David said unto Saul, Thy servant kept his father's sheep, and there came a lion, and a bear, and took a lamb out of the flock:

35. And I went out after him, and smote him, and delivered it out of his mouth: and when he arose against me, I caught him by his beard, and smote him, and slew him.

36. Thy servant slew both the lion and the bear: and this uncircumcised Philistine shall be as one of them, seeing he hath defied the armies of the living God.

Let me share one of my victories that I have had to remind myself of several times. I call it the ten-dollar miracle. I knew that our bank account was getting low so I went and got a printout from the bank. I had "0" money and a five dollar check still out that would probably go through that night. I sat down on the wall that went around the flagpole at the car lot where I was working as a salesperson. (Which was why I did not have any money in the bank, I cannot sell cars.) I sat there and prayed, I told God that I was going to believe Him for ten dollars that day. I got up and caught the next customer and while they were out test driving the car a friend came out and ask me if I could close for him that night, he said "Randy I'll give you ten dollars to close in my place tonight." I said "okay" he handed me the ten dollars. "I sure need to get this money to the bank before it closes" I told my friend. He said "I'll stand right here and watch for your customers and keep them company till you get back." I got back before they did and they bought the car. I walked back to my office, and there sat the manager with a previous customer of mine. They wanted to trade in their SUV for a truck. I was with them until closing time, so I would have been there anyway, without filling in for my friend. Like the cavalry, God came to the rescue, got there just in the nick of time and saved me from an overdraft at the bank. Now every time I have financial problems I remember my ten-dollar miracle and know that if God did it once He will do it again.

What is better than that is the Bible tells me that God is no respecter of persons, what He did for David He will do for me.

40. And he took his staff in his hand, and chose him five smooth stones out of the brook, and put them in a shepherd's bag which he had, even in a scrip; and his sling was in his hand: and he drew near to the Philistine.

Many people have wondered why David picked up five smooth stones, there have been a lot of sermons preached on the subject and a lot of speculation some will tell you that Goliath had four brothers, some will tell you that faith has five letters in it. I believe that David was preparing for a fight. That he did not know he would knock down the giant with one stone, it might take five. Becoming a Christian does not mean that you will not face battles; it does, however, mean that God will be with you and bring you through those battles. Solutions may not be easy, but they will come if you just don't shoot the horse.

48. And it came to pass, when the Philistine arose, and came, and drew nigh to meet David, that David hasted, and ran toward the army to meet the Philistine.

49. And David put his hand in his bag, and took thence a stone, and slang it, and smote the Philistine in his forehead, that the stone sunk into his forehead; and he fell upon his face to the earth.

50. So David prevailed over the Philistine with a sling and with a stone, and smote the Philistine, and slew him; but there was no sword in the hand of David.

51. Therefore David ran, and stood upon the Philistine, and took his sword, and drew it out of the sheath thereof, and slew him, and cut off his head therewith.

And when the Philistines saw their champion was dead, they fled. David brought down the giant with a stone, but that was not enough. He ran and climbed on top on the fallen Goliath and using the giant's own sword, cut off his head. There are many times we overcome problems only to have them to rear their ugly heads again, we need to do as David did, get on top of the problem and use the Bible as our sword, and cut the head off that thing. In other words, learn to keep your victories by staying in the word.

So when problems come, solve them, work through them, believe in a loving God who wants to help, just don't shoot the horse.

Chapter 2

Yelling into the refrigerator

One afternoon I was sitting at the table in our breakfast room when my wife walked through going to the kitchen. There is a large opening between the two rooms so I could see what my wife was doing. She went to the refrigerator, opened the door and as she was looking inside she yelled our daughter's name, "Erica!". I said, "honey, she's not in there!" If I had simply, gone on the information that I saw that day I would have called the doctors with the special coat and reminded God that He has given us a sound mind. However, what actually happened is my wife had been in Erica's room and asked her what she wanted to eat. Erica told her macaroni and cheese. My wife went to the refrigerator and discovered that there wasn't any. She was calling to Erica to tell her there was no macaroni. I was relieved to find that she was not going crazy; she had just lost her noodles.

There have been many situational comedies written over the years in which, the whole premise of the story is based on someone jumping to the wrong conclusion. Have you ever heard of someone jumping to the right conclusion? Probably not, however, there have been many problems, broken hearts, disappointments and wrecked lives caused by jumping from few facts to a wrong conclusion.

One of the devils' greatest advantages in causing us problems is our propensity to jump to conclusions.

2nd Corinthians 10: 5. Casting down imaginations, and every high thing that exalteth itself against the knowledge of God, and bringing into captivity every thought to the obedience of Christ;

2nd Corinthians 2:11. Lest Satan should get an advantage of us: for we are not ignorant of his devices.

The word *thought* in second Corinthians 10:5 and the word *devices* in Second Corinthians 2:11 happen to be the same word, *noema*.

Is it possible that we are told to bring into captivity every thought because thoughts are a device of the devil? Of course they are. I am shocked at what some people imagine. I have had dreams that some of these horror writers would like to hear.

When our children are late coming home, we can imagine some pretty bad things. A late night telephone call can spark many fearful thoughts in the short time it takes to reach for the receiver. Sometimes Satan will help out with a string of thoughts.

The telephone rings and wife answers, only to have the other party hang up. *Thought:* "If a woman answers, hang up." Then that wife finds a telephone number in his pocket. *Thought:* "I wonder if this is who called." Next, she sees him speaking to a woman outside his work place. *Thought*: "I knew something was going on."

What was going on? The call was a wrong number, the telephone number was actually his bank pin number he had put a prefix in front of it so it would look like a telephone number and not a PIN. The woman who was speaking to him outside of his work was asking directions. He is in a lot of trouble and does not even know it. Why? Because that cartoon character of a devil sitting on one shoulder was actually there whispering; "If a woman answers, hang up, I wonder if this is who called, and I knew something was going on".

One Halloween my wife, who is a makeup artist, fixed herself up to look like Liz Taylor. We had gone to Wal-Mart for a few things and some friends saw us in the parking lot speaking to someone. "I wonder who that is with Brother Randy," The daughter asked. The mother replied," Oh, I'm sure it's his cousin". Then my wife and I started walking into the store holding hands. Our friends went into shock! Fortunately, the person we were speaking to explained it to them and we also bumped into them in the store later. There was another Friend who saw us, went home and told her mother" I don't know who that woman was that was with Randy". We also got that straightened out. I do not know who else saw us but I do know that next Halloween we will not be going to Wal-Mart. The devil was busy slinging *noemas* around that night.

A college professor once said, "There is always at least one fact in every case that you do not know". It would be good for us to remember that. It may be one of the reasons that Jesus tells us to "JUDGE NOT".

Jumping to conclusions is like shooting the horse, taking action before we know all the facts.

There was a strip joint on the highway not far from the where we live and I would drive by it and pray for the place to close. One day my wife and I were driving to town and as we passed this club I noticed that the roof had a very large black place on it, thinking that it had caught fire and would not be in operation I said "WELL GOOD!" my wife did not see the same thing that I had. She saw a sign on the side of the road saying "BIKINI CAR WASH SATURDAY." Guess who jumped to a conclusion that day?

Our imagination can be used against us, even to the point of causing the downfall of, and destruction of humankind.

> *5. And God saw that the wickedness of man was great in the earth, and that every imagination of the thoughts of his heart was only evil continually.*
>
> *6. And it repented the Lord that he had made man on the earth, and it grieved him at his heart. 7. And the Lord said, I will destroy man whom I have created from the face of the earth. Genesis 6:5-7*

Just IMAGINE what could happen if we turned our thoughts toward God. What if we let Him feed our dreams, fuel our thoughts and ignite our imagination? If we could imagine ourselves witnessing, praying for the sick, seeing people healed, walking with God daily, just being like Jesus, can you imagine the impact it would have on our lives and the lives of every one we meet.

Read the following scriptures and see if all this is possible.

> *Philippians 4:8 Finally, brethren, whatsoever things are true, whatsoever things are honest, whatsoever things are just, whatsoever things are pure, whatso-*

ever things are lovely, whatsoever things are of good report; if there be any virtue, and if there be any praise, think on these things.

Ephesians 3:20 Now unto him that is able to do exceeding abundantly above all that we ask or think, according to the power that worketh in us,

If our thoughts are only good, then the conclusions that we may on occasion jump to could only be a good.

Chapter 3

When Words Fall Short

§

My daughter Erica was a good basketball player in high school. She could make a shot from the three-point line most of the time. I had to stop playing HORSE with her. I also have a niece that was very little, not quite three feet tall and would not weigh fifty pounds if she were soaking wet and had her pockets full of rocks. My niece would come over to our house and would insist on taking her turn at shooting. She would take the basketball in both hands, lower it between her legs and sling it with all her might. The ball would fall short of the goal everytime. No matter how hard she tried, she just was not big enough to reach the goal.

There are times in out lives when no matter how hard we try to counsel, comfort or enlighten, our words, just like that basketball, fall short of our goal. We simply are not strong enough or wise enough to reach it.

When I was a children's pastor, many years ago, the children's church was in an upstairs room with the back door leading outside. One Sunday after the service, I cleaned up and left through the back door. About half way down the stairs sat a little girl about eight years old named Annie (named changed). She had her elbows propped on her knees and her head cradled in her hands. I sat down beside her, and asked, "Annie, what's the matter?" With out looking up she said, "my daddy shot himself this morning." I knew that any words I might speak would fall short at that moment. There was nothing I could say that could ease the pain she was feeling.

There was another time when words fell short. I got the call late one night that my cousin had died in an automobile accident. It took me about six hours to make the drive and I spent the time contemplating what I would say to my aunt. Before I reached my destination I felt that I had come up with the perfect words of wisdom and comfort, I was going to make everything okay for my aunt. When I walked into the room where she was sitting she looked up at me and said, "oh Randy what are we going to do?" I sat down beside her and shared those perfect words of wisdom and comfort with her. I knew that I was helping her and that she would be all right. When I finished, I felt that I needed a good pat on the back when someone else walked into the room and she looked up at them and said, "Oh, what are we going to do?" She did not hear my words! They were not strong enough to penetrate the pain and the confusion in her heart and mind. They fell short.

As I sat next to Annie, I knew that any words I might come up with would not help. Her hurt was to deep, her confusion to great and her questions to many, and I just was not big enough. Yet I had to do something. The only thing I knew to do was simply reach out and put my arms around that little girl. I held her until her grandmother came, and picked her up.

Galatians 6:2. Bear ye one another's burdens, and so fulfill the law of Christ.

How do we bear one another's burdens? What is a burden? A burden is a weight that has to be carried.? Anything that weighs us down qualifies as a burden . It could be a problem to which we can find no solution. It could be a disappointment or a deep hurt. That may be why we use the phrase a heavy heart. Annie had a very heavy heart that morning. Words could not lighten the weight but sometimes just being there, offering a comforting presence, helps make the weight a little lighter. Making the weight lighter for the hurting fulfils the law of Christ. The law of Christ here figuratively means a principle. We fulfill the principles of Christ by being there for the hurting, letting them feel your strength, your caring and love. Every moment we give a little relief is a moment closer to the healing of the hurt.

There may be times in our lives when the circumstances are too many and the situation too great for us to find comfort in words. No matter how great the words may be they simply fall short. What do we do in times like these? We sit down and let a great big loving God with strong comforting arms hold us until things get better.

Psalms 139: 7-10 Whither shall I go from thy spirit? or whither shall I flee from thy presence?

8. If I ascend up into heaven, thou art there: if I make my bed in hell, behold, thou art there.

9. If I take the wings of the morning, and dwell in the uttermost parts of the sea;

10. Even there shall thy hand lead me, ***and thy right hand shall hold me.***

Sometimes when there are no words that will comfort, just the simple act of being there gives strength for that person to heal and rebuild their lives.

Bear ye one another's burdens, and so fulfil the law of Christ. (Galatians 6:2)

Remember the song we sang in Children's Church, "When we all pull together, how happy we'll be. When your friends are my friends and my friends are God's friends, when we all pull together how happy we will be." We are all in this together and have strength in each other, because we have God in us and being there for others will let God shine in us.

Chapter 4

What happened to the fish?

I told the story of Noah's Ark to a kindergarten class one day. When I explained that every thing on the earth had drowned in the flood one little four year old girl raised her hand and asked, "What happened to the fish?" I had never thought of that and this little girl in all her innocence made my bible college degree shrink to the size of a postage stamp. I am sure that all of you know the answer to her question, but for the ones of you who do not.

> *Genesis 7: 21. And all flesh died that moved upon the earth, both of fowl, and of cattle, and of beast, and of every creeping thing that creepeth upon the earth, and every man:*
>
> *22. All in whose nostrils was the breath of life, of all that was in the dry land, died.*

What I had experience that day before a classroom of four year olds was HUMILITY.

HUMILITY — *a freedom from arrogance that grows out of the recognition that all we have and are comes from God (Nelson's New Bible Dictionary)*

I once heard a story of a man who died in the Jamestown flood, when he got to heaven he was excited about getting the chance to share his experience with everyone. He was nagging Peter for his chance to "testify" to all the saints, and Peter kept assuring the man that he would get his chance. Mr. Jamestown kept persisting until Peter finally gave in and said, "Okay you can testify, but remember one thing, Noah is here."

It does not matter how big you are or how great your accomplishments are, there is always someone that has soared to greater heights. What we have to remember is that the only way we are able to climb to those heights is on the ladder of God's grace. In fact, it is more like an escalator because all we do is step on and God does the work. All we have to do is be available and willing, and God will accomplish things through us.

Mother Teresa is a great example of humility. India will never be the same because she walked its streets and loved its people. And yet when asked about her accomplishments, Mother Teresa, who one day may be considered a saint, said, "I am just an instrument in the hand of a mighty God"

The Greek philosophers hated the concept of humility; they thought it showed a person's inadequacy, or that a humble person had no dignity. But a person who realizes where his strength comes from is not inadequate but wise.

The greatest example of true humility would, of course, be our savior Jesus. John tells us He was in the beginning with God. [3]All things were made through Him, and without Him nothing was made that were made. John 1:2&3

Jesus the creator of the universe, ⁶Who, being in the form of God, thought it not robbery to be equal with God: ⁷But made himself of no reputation, and took upon him the form of a servant, and was made in the likeness of men: ⁸And being found in fashion as a man, he humbled himself, and became obedient unto death, even the death of the cross. Philippians 2:6-8

The greatest that was ever born, choose to be born in a stable. The one who formed the universe lay in a manger. The one who created man became a baby. The one who breathed life into man gave up his own life on a cross. The one who gave us the Ten Commandments died with outlaws. Who among man could have swallowed his pride the way Jesus did. It is something that we must do, we must take up the cross daily, and we must crucify ourself. A forgotten tradition in the Church is the foot washing service, is it mandatory? This is another question for the theologians. I was in such a service one night and was a little hesitant to participate, but something inside me gave a gentle push to join in. There was a man there that I worked with and we had some words earlier. That gentle push was toward him. I knelt in front of him and began to wash his feet. He sat in his chair and cried like a baby. It did not matter who was right or wrong when our pride was crucified.

Jesus came to this earth in the form of a man, to be crucified. We do a lot of things to be like Jesus, therefore, to be like Jesus we need to start with a crucifixion. When we crucify our pride then humility can take over and we will realize that what we have and what we are, is because of the grace of God.

I saw two different preachers on TV; both seem to have miracles operate in their services. One, after praying for a woman, told her to open her eyes and look at the man of God. The other, told a woman that it was not him, that he was not anything, but God had touched her and to praise God. I will not judge the two preachers (cannot judge) but I can determine which one knows the source of all miracles and which one points to Jesus. Both men may have been sincere, one was just sincerely wrong.

The fear of the Lord is the instruction of wisdom; and before honour is humility. Proverbs 15:33

Humility is not a bad thing; in fact, it is probably one of the keys to finding the blessings of God.

By humility and the fear of the Lord are riches, and honour, and life. Proverbs 22:4

Do not be afraid of things that helps to humble you, they may be blessings from God to help bring you to a closer relationship with the Father. Many people are looking for God to bless them with riches and honor and abundant life. I cannot promise you any of these things but if that is your quest, you should start with humility. When you gain true humility these other things are not an issue. When they stop being an issue then God can bless you with those things.

Likewise, ye younger, submit yourselves unto the elder. Yea, all of you be subject one to another, and be clothed with humility: for God resisteth the proud, and giveth grace to the humble. 1st Peter 5:5

It is only by the Grace of God that we become anything, reach any heights, and attain any goals.

God gives that grace to the humble.

Chapter 5

It should not happen this way

I won the opportunity to play again,……..again. The label around the soft drink said one in twelve wins. Someone else must have drunk my drink, because my twelfth bottle cap read, "Please play again". I have gotten where I prefer the drinks with no contest, just blank caps, and no disappointments. The only problem with the blank cap drink is, no expectation. You know you are getting the drink, after all, you paid for it, but the possibility of a free prize keeps us buying and looking under the cap.

Life is full of disappointments. Opening the Christmas present to find pajamas is a disappointment, but we still wait for Christmas morning and the chance to open gifts. Disappointments and surprises, mountains and valleys, day and night, cold and warmth, one makes the other worthwhile. One makes the other appreciated.

Disappointment Street may be a long one but if you keep on it you will eventually reach the end. You may even notice some of the streets that veer off: Goodtime Avenue, Delight

Road, Peaceful Highway, Believers Boulevard, or Heavenly Parkway. There are many turns that will put Disappointment Street behind you, and happiness ahead, so keep driving.

If you have suffered disappointment in your life you do not stand on the street alone. Some great Bible heroes traveled that same street, expecting great things that just did not happen.

Joseph expected to find a mighty ruler under his cap but found slavery instead.. Jonah thought he would find God's righteous judgment under his cap, but what he found was God's divine forgiveness. The prodigal son thought he would find adventure under his cap but instead found destitution. There are many others in the bible that when faced with disappointment, trusted in God, and their disappointment was turned into victory.

The story of Joseph can be read in the time it takes to read this chapter but the story actually covers many years. Things did not turn around for him in an instant but over time. If there was ever a dysfunctional family in the Bible, it has to be Joseph's. Jacob had two wives, one that he loved very deeply and one that he was just married to. The wife that he loved was the mother of Joseph, so Joseph was more special to Jacob than any of his other children. When Jacob took his family back to his home land he was afraid of the confrontation he would have with his brother Easu. So he divided his caravan up and sent the maids and their children first, then Leah and her children. Bringing up the rear, was Joseph and Rachel. You know that had to make the other children feel very special. When Joseph was in the fields shepherding with his brothers he reported back to his father an "ill report" about his brothers. Joseph was a tell-a-tale.

Now Israel loved Joseph more than all his children, because he was the son of his old age: and he made him a coat of many colours (Genesis 37:3)

Jacob showed favoritism for Joseph and Joseph showed a spoiled attitude and his brothers learned to show hatred for Joseph. The coat of many colors was a coat of nobility, stating that Joseph would one day be the ruler of his family, which did not sit very well with his brothers. Joseph did not let his brothers' jealousy stop him from flaunting the fact that he was special before them.

His brothers of course noticed their father's partiality, and consequently hated Joseph; they couldn't say a kind word to him.

One night Joseph had a dream and promptly reported the details to his brothers, causing even deeper hatred.

``Listen to this,'' he proudly announced.

``We were out in the field binding sheaves, and my sheaf stood up, and your sheaves all gathered around it and bowed low before it!''

``So you want to be our king, do you?'' his brothers derided. And they hated him both for the dream and for his cocky attitude.

Then he had another dream and told it to his brothers. ``Listen to my latest dream,'' he boasted. ``The sun, moon, and eleven stars bowed low before me!''

This time he told his father as well as his brothers; but his father rebuked him. ``What is this?'' he asked. ``Shall I indeed, and your mother and brothers come and bow before you?''

His brothers were fit to be tied concerning this affair, but his father gave it quite a bit of thought and wondered what it all meant. (Genesis 37:4-11 Living Bible)

When Joseph opened his special bottle cap he thought there would be "Ruler" under it, but things did not turn out as he had expected. The first chance his brothers had, they took care of the problem of Joseph.

When they saw him coming, recognizing him in the distance, they decided to kill him! "Here comes that master-dreamer," they exclaimed. ``Come on, let's kill him and toss him into a well and tell father that a wild animal has eaten him. Then we'll see what will become of all his dreams!''

But Reuben hoped to spare Joseph's life. ``Let's not kill him,'' he said; ``we'll shed no blood--let's throw him alive into this well here; that way he'll die without our touching him!'' (Reuben was planning to get him out later and return him to his father.)

So when Joseph got there, they pulled off his brightly-colored robe,

and threw him into an empty well--there was no water in it.

Then they sat down for supper. Suddenly they noticed a string of camels coming towards them in the distance, probably Ishmaelite traders who were taking gum, spices, and herbs from Gilead to Egypt.

``Look there,'' Judah said to the others. ``Here come some Ishmaelites. Let's sell Joseph to them! Why kill him and have a guilty conscience? Let's not be responsible for his death, for, after all, he is our brother!'' And his brothers agreed.

So when the traders came by, his brothers pulled Joseph out of the well and sold him to them for twenty pieces of silver, and they took him along to Egypt. (Genesis 37:16-28 Living Bible)

Joseph found slavery, not ruler. Things did not turn out like he had planned, but Joseph hung in there with God and God brought about His plan in His time but it was not overnight. Joseph was seventeen when he was sold as a slave and around thirty when his brothers came to Egypt seeking food. Joseph suffered great disappointment in his family who had betrayed him.

Jonah, when he looked under his cap thought there would be righteous judgment for the people of Nineveh instead there was forgiveness for a very wicked people.

Jonah was sent to Nineveh by God to preach their approaching destruction. When a city becomes so wicked that God is willing to destroy it, then it is a city that a man of God would be afraid to enter. Jonah did not want to go to Nineveh; in fact, he was afraid to go to Nineveh, so he ran and headed in the other direction. God always has the means to get people where He wants them. God prepared a great fish to transport Jonah to Nineveh, some people think that a person could not survive for three days in the belly of a whale, but this whale was prepared by God to take Jonah there. Jonah went to

Nineveh to preach judgment, and the people repented. God forgave them and did not destroy the city. Most preachers would love to see an entire city repent after delivering a sermon, but Jonah was disappointed. He preached that they would be destroyed but God forgave. This made him look bad because his words did not come true. Jonah went outside the city and a vine grew up to offer a shade from the scorching sun, but God allowed a worm to come and destroy the vine. Jonah complained to God about the vine and God showed him that he was showing more mercy to a vine than one hundred and twenty thousand people.

Jonah felt disappointment in God.

Next is the prodigal son who found disappointment in himself.

Hoping to find great adventure under his cap instead found destitution.

``A man had two sons. When the younger told his father, `I want my share of your estate now, instead of waiting until you die!' his father agreed to divide his wealth between his sons. ``A few days later this younger son packed all his belongings and took a trip to a distant land, and there wasted all his money on parties and prostitutes. About the time his money was gone a great famine swept over the land, and he began to starve.

He persuaded a local farmer to hire him to feed his pigs.

The boy became so hungry that even the pods he was feeding the swine looked good to him and no one gave him anything.

``When he finally came to his senses, he said to himself, `At home even the hired men have food enough and to spare, and here I am, dying of hunger! (Matthew 15: 11-17--Living Bible.)

The best part of the story is that when "he finally came to his senses, he went home, where even the servants were treated better than he was treating himself. When he got just down the road from his home his father recognized him, ran to him, gave him a big hug, kiss, and said welcome home.

No matter how far from God we go He is standing and waiting for us to come home, and when we make that turn He runs to us to embrace us and welcomes us home.

Joseph was disappointed in his brothers, Jonah was disappointed in God and the prodigal son became disappointed in himself. You may be disappointed in family, God or yourself or maybe your job, friends, of how life has turned out in general. The answer is simple, give yourself to God, He can turn things around. God can turn disappointments to prizes.

Keep opening those bottle caps, one day you will find a "you win". Just don't shoot the horse.

Chapter 6

Christ Like In Short Shorts

§

This is the story of two women who came across my path at about the same time and taught me a valuable lesson. The first was a young woman who stopped by the mission that I was serving as chaplain, she was dressed in a tee shirt and jeans that were cut off fairly short. The second woman was dressed in a long dress and had her hair all pinned up in a little ball on top of her head, she carried herself like one of the Pentecostal women in the community that I really admire.

The first young woman came into the mission seeking help with food; she had her little five-year old daughter with her. I always made it a practice to ask people who came to the mission for one reason or another if they knew Jesus as their personal Lord and Savior. When I asked this young lady the biggest grin spread across her face and she said," yes He's my savior". It was lunchtime at the mission and when I brought them the bags of food, I invited them to stay for for the meal. I looked at the little girl and said, "We're having sloppy joes, she looked up at her mother with anticipation in her eyes and her mom said okay. They went into the lunchroom where a line had already formed. I usually had to keep a watch on the food to ensure that some people did not take too much and there not be enough for everyone. When this mother and daughter came to the serving table, she barely got enough for her and her daughter to have a sandwich each. They quietly went to a table and bowed their heads and said a prayer over the food. When they had finished their meal they lingered around until every one had departed and she thanked me for the food and offered to wash all the dishes that had been used that day. I told her that we had a dishwasher and that everything was taken care of. As she left, I could not help but to think of the story in the book of Genesis of Rachel offering to water all of the camels. .

The second woman was the perfect picture of one who lived a very strict life. I met her on a day when there was a big jamboree going on in town and there was no parking for the businesses that were open that day. The Mission store had its own parking lot but it began to fill quickly with people going up town for the jamboree. One of our workers, Mark, went outside to explain to people that the parking spaces were for store customers only. A van pulled into one of the parking spaces and this saintly looking little woman got out and headed for the sidewalk going away from the store. Mark approached her and said, "Excuse me maam but these parking spaces are reserved for the store." That little woman turned on him, started cursing him, and told him that she would never shop in that store. Mark just stood there with his mouth open, as she climbed into her van and drove off. Mark walked into the store with eyes wide and said," She cursed me out!"

We are taught that we should not judge people, but if we were to put the girl in short shorts and the "saintly dressed" woman side by side and ask which one was a Christian we would, judging by appearance, choose the "saintly dressed" woman. However, if we were to just describe their actions without seeing them and ask which one was a Christian we would choose the girl in short shorts.

John 7:24 [24]Judge not according to the appearance, but judge righteous judgment.

It is not so much what we wear that shows what we are. I know that we are supposed to dress for success, and many times how we dress is very important. I just have a hard time picturing the disciples wearing "I'm a Jesus freak" Tee shirt, sporting I love Jesus ball caps, and having a little fish stuck on the hip of their donkeys. I do think that they wore the attitude of Christ, and that was why they were called Christians.

Someone once told me that if you were to see a lawyer and a politician and a preacher walking together you would not be able to tell which one was the preacher. The question might be asked then, what should a Christian wear? If a Christian is to wear anything that would distinguish them from the world it should be the things you can see with the heart.

I will greatly rejoice in the Lord, my soul shall be joyful in my God; for he hath clothed me with the garments of salvation, he hath covered me with the robe of righteousness, as a bridegroom decketh himself with ornaments, and as a bride adorneth herself with her jewels. Isaiah 61:10

You should wear your salvation like a bride wearing jewels. Your salvation should stand out and shine like gold and diamonds. I have performed many weddings, and it is an awesome sight to see the Groom come out wearing his Tux and stand at the front of the church tall, straight and proud, and if you listen carefully you can actually hear some people take in a breath when the bride walks down the aisle. Our salvation and righteousness should be worn like a brides gown because when we walk all eyes will be on us.

Likewise, ye younger, submit yourselves unto the elder. Yea, all of you be subject one to another, and be clothed with humility First Peter 5:5

While we should be proud that we are saved and headed for heaven it is important to also wear our salvation with humility.

I will never forget the girl in short shorts, not because of the shorts but because of the smile on her face and the sparkle in her eyes when she said, "Jesus is my savior".

Chapter 7

Beyond the shadow of a cloud

§

The mother got the call late one night that her son had been in an auto accident at willow creek. She ran to her car and got to the site before the rescue team. Her son sat behind the wheel unable to speak but able to blink his eyes to her questions. The rescue squad arrived and took him to the emergency room where he slipped into unconsciousness then into eternity. The day of the funeral was a wet one, the sky was completely hidden by a blanket of gray clouds that sent a constant drizzle to the soaking ground. The question lingered in the mother's heart of the condition of her son's soul. He knew about the Gospel and the plan of salvation, but she did not know about his commitment. He was conscience for a while and in his last moments could have made a decision for Christ. The thief on the cross did and was in paradise that very day. However, what about the son, the mother needed to know something. When the last words were spoken at the service and the family was exiting the church, the mother needed and longed for a sign. She stepped out into the weather and the sun broke through the clouds and was shining down on the little area where she and some others stood. A sign, God had given this mother hope.

Hosea 2:15. There I will give back her vineyards to her, and transform her Valley of Troubles into a Door of Hope. She will respond to me there, singing with joy as in days long ago in her youth, after I had freed her from captivity in Egypt. (Living Bible)

God can turn our valleys of trouble into doors of hope. It does not matter what the valley is what matters is that God will lead us through the valley, or put a door in the valley. He has promised that we will not be put through more than we are able to bear but with the temptation would make a way of escape. (1st Corinthains 10:13) That way of escape is the door of hope.

Hosea 2:15 refers to Israel and Christians and their relationship with God. It is beautifully painted in the story of Hosea and his wife Gomer. Gomer was a temple prostitute and God told Hosea to go and marry her. Hosea's name means salvation, so here is salvation taking a prostitute for a wife. I image people would laugh at Hosea and many criticized him for what he was doing. Hosea would look them straight in the eye and say how you can judge me when you belong to God and yet worship all those other gods. I may have taken a temple prostitute for a wife but you have taken the god of the temple for your god. Then Hosea and Gomer had children, the first they named Jezreel which means "God will sow" the next child was named Lo-ruhamah, which means "no more mercy" then the third, was named Lo-ammi which means "not mine". Do you think that the people were saying, "What were you thinking Hosea naming your children names like that"? Hosea would reply, "Israel will experience Jezreel, you will sow what you are reaping and God will not have mercy on you because you are no longer His." When things started going bad for Gomer, as with anyone who steps away from God and His will, Gomer ended up on the slave block, everything lost, with no control over her destiny. Then came along salvation (Hosea) and bought her back. She was his and he bought her. Remind you of anyone. We belong to God and sell ourselves to anything that comes along, our indiscretions cause us to become slaves to our desires and Salvation comes and buys us back. There is always hope in God. The definition of hope is *confident trust that something will happen*. It does not matter what we go through, what matters is that we go through them with God. He will never let us down. The Bible tells us that God will never leave or forsake us, that God will be with us until the end of the age, and then we will be with Him.

Hope for a child is wishful thinking, hoping that Santa will bring that special gift, or that it will snow for Christmas. Maybe this weekend we will get to go to the beach. Daddy will come home early, or momma will prepare that special desert for dinner. Some adults have the same kind of wishful thinking hope. "Maybe we will win the lottery" or "maybe it will snow for Christmas". Sometimes children and adults have the same kind of hope.

The Christian however has a different kind of hope. Confident trust that something will happen. The Christian has comfort because of his confident trust in God to make something happen. With God, there is hope for the discouraged, deliverance for the bound, healing for the sick. Read some of the promises in the Bible, they are yours. Read the blessings in the Bible, they are yours.

> *"And if you obey the voice of the Lord your God, being careful to do all his commandments which I*

command you this day, the Lord your God will set you high above all the nations of the earth.

And all these blessings shall come upon you and overtake you, if you obey the voice of the Lord your God.

Blessed shall you be in the city, and blessed shall you be in the field.

Blessed shall be the fruit of your body, and the fruit of your ground, and the fruit of your beasts, the increase of your cattle, and the young of your flock.

Blessed shall be your basket and your kneading-trough.

Blessed shall you be when you come in, and blessed shall you be when you go out.

"The Lord will cause your enemies who rise against you to be defeated before you; they shall come out against you one way, and flee before you seven ways.

The Lord will command the blessing upon you in your barns, and in all that you undertake; and he will bless you in the land which the Lord your God gives you. (Revised Standard Version, Deuteronomy 28:1-8)

What is hope to the Christian? Maybe it is faith. Knowing that God will make all things work together for your good. Knowing that God wishes to bless you beyond measure, if you will just obey Him and keep the commandments. The commandments are there for our benefit and because God loves us and only wants what is best for us. When hard times come on us we look to God. Why not look to God before the hard times, maybe they will not come, and if they do, we are ahead of the game because we are already looking to God.

Why art thou cast down, O my soul? and why art thou disquieted in me? hope thou in God: for I shall yet praise him for the help of his countenance. Psalms 42:5

The Hebrew word countenance, translated, is face. The literal translation for "the help of His countenance" is "the salvation of His face". Have you ever pictured God looking down from heaven and seeing you and what is going on in your life? I do. I believe God is watching, just like he saw the disciples toiling in the sea and walked on water to go to them, He sees us and comes whenever we need help, or just want to talk. He will be there just like when He looked down on that mother as she walked out of the church, with His face shining, and giving hope.

Chapter 8

Raped by bitterness

I sat in front of the desk of an executive as she told me how much she hated a certain young man who used to date her daughter. She told me "If I saw him standing on the side of the road, I would run off the road and run him over". I said "Carol, (names changed) you've got to get over this, you've got to forgive him". She looked down at the paper work on her desk and when she looked back up at me she had tears in her eyes and said, "He raped her". I did not know what to say at that moment because I also have a daughter, and I am a little afraid of how I would handle it if the circumstances were mine and not hers. What is really sad is that the daughter was able to put her life back together but the mother was not. There was more then one rape. The daughter, raped by a boyfriend, the mother by bitterness. What is bitterness?

Causing pain or grief; hard to admit or bear. (SYN) painful, distressing, grievous. (World Book Dictionary)

What does bitterness mean to a Christian? Bitterness can interfere with a Christian's relationship with God. Bitterness can block communication between the Father and His children. When a person lets their heart be filled with bitterness and their mind is troubled with the pain that caused it, there is seldom room for the warmth of a loving Savior. The Bible tells us that "as a man thinks in his heart so is he" that would tell me that a person whose thoughts are full of bitterness will become a bitter person. Anything that comes between you and God becomes a sin. What kind of blessings do bitter people miss out on because of their bitterness? What about peace, can bitterness and peace co-exist side by side? I do not think so. If peace is to be free from all strife, then how can a troubled mind experience peace? *Peace I leave with you, my peace I give unto you.* Peace is a wonderful gift from God and bitterness drives it from us like opposing magnets. To let God have His way in our lives we have to expel bitterness from from it

> *Hebrews 12:15. Looking diligently lest any man fail of the grace of God; lest any root of bitterness springing up trouble you, and thereby many be defiled;*

The wrong root in a garden can grow into something very big; it can take over the whole garden, choking out the fruit. The root of bitterness can grow and choke out the fruit of the Spirit. The fruit of the Spirit is love, joy, peace, patience, kindness, goodness, faithfulness, gentleness, and self-control. Those are some pretty important attributes to lose for the sake of bitterness.

If bitterness is allowed to continue in our lives, then other things will also crop up in our lives. Bitterness will slowly grow into hate, creating a hateful person. Hatred will grow into cruelty, making a cruel person. Is a Christian supposed to be bitter, hateful and cruel? A Christian is to be kind to one another tender hearted, and forgiving.

How does a person become bitter and how do they overcome? The seed that grows into the root of bitterness is unforgiveness. Every one goes through hard times and hurtful times. To make it through life without hurt is to not live at all. To suffer hurt and not forgive is to suffer damage to your spirit, pollution to your soul, poison to your attitude, and death unto your witness. Unforgiveness is possibly one of the greatest weapons that Satan uses against the Christian.

Matthew 6:14-15

14. For if ye forgive men their trespasses, your heavenly Father will also forgive you:

15. But if ye forgive not men their trespasses, neither will your Father forgive your trespasses.

If a Christian cannot forgive, what will happen when they face God. I do not want to face God with the sin of unforgiveness. Do you? Jesus offers this story on unforgiveness; I share it with you from "The Living Bible"

``The Kingdom of Heaven can be compared to a king who decided to bring his accounts up to date.

In the process, one of his debtors was brought in who owed him $10,000,000!

He couldn't pay, so the king ordered him sold for the debt, also his wife and children and everything he had.

``But the man fell down before the king, his face in the dust, and said, `Oh, sir, be patient with me and I will pay it all.'

``Then the king was filled with pity for him and released him and forgave his debt.

``But when the man left the king, he went to a man who owed him $2,000 and grabbed him by the throat and demanded instant payment.

``The man fell down before him and begged him to give him a little time. `Be patient and I will pay it,' he pled.

``But his creditor wouldn't wait. He had the man arrested and jailed until the debt would be paid in full.

``Then the man's friends went to the king and told him what had happened.

And the king called before him the man he had forgiven and said, `You evil-hearted wretch! Here I forgave you all that tremendous debt, just because you asked me to--

shouldn't you have mercy on others, just as I had mercy on you?'

``Then the angry king sent the man to the torture chamber until he had paid every last penny due.

So shall my heavenly Father do to you if you refuse to truly forgive your brothers.''

This is a hard lesson, but God wants us to grow to be like Christ, the disciples were so much like Jesus that they were called "Christ like". During the last days of Jesus he witnessed the people turn against him, betray him, and lie about him. Jesus heard his own people yelling "crucify him, crucify him." He was beaten, whipped, and nailed to a cross, and as he hung on that cross he prayed, "Father forgive them, for they do not know what they are doing". If Jesus could do that, is it to much for Him to condemn unforgiveness?

In John chapter fifteen verse twelve, Jesus makes this statement *"this is my commandment, That ye love one another, as I have loved you."* In addition, in John fourteen and twenty-four Jesus tells us *"He that loveth me not keepeth not my sayings."* These two verses lets us know that unforgiveness shows that we do not love Jesus as we should. Unforgiveness also hinders our physical and emotional health. If you hold on to unforgivness, you continue to feel the pain of the offense. When others commit an offense similar to yours, it renews the hurt of the original offense. Soon you find that others with similar hurts are keeping company with you, and the hurt is the topic of conversation. The saying that misery loves company is true but how can a person's wounds heal when they are continually being opened? How can you put your mind on the things of God when you are continually thinking of a hurt? You cannot. How good can it be for you to ponder hurts for long periods of time? If you constantly think of hurtful things, the body will soon be affected and react to the hurt, the body becomes less strong to resist or fight off disease. Why then would a person hold on to unforgiveness? Because many times we feel that it is our right to hold on to the offense and withhold forgiveness. We often feel that the offender does not deserve our forgiveness. Forgiveness should be given even if never asked for. Forgiveness will not make an unrepentant person right, but it will make the offended one right and set them on the road to recovery.

Forgiveness:

Learning to forgive will give you freedom, freedom from hurt, freedom from resentment, freedom from the need to retaliate, freedom to heal, freedom to move on and start living your life, freedom to be the person that God intended you to be.

One of the greatest stories in the Bible about forgiveness is the story of Joseph. We looked at Joseph in the chapter on disappointments, now we will look at him from the perspective of forgiveness. You can read the story of Joseph in a few minutes but the story actually takes place over several years. Joseph was, as I mentioned earlier, from a dysfunctional family. His father treated his children differently. There was jealousy between brothers. The brothers had different mothers, and there were a lot of misunderstandings that lead to a lot of drama in the family.

Jacob's son Joseph was now seventeen years old. His job, along with his half-brothers, the sons of his father's wives Bilhah and Zilpah, was to shepherd his father's flocks. But Joseph reported to his father some of the bad things they were doing.

Now as it happened, Israel loved Joseph more than any of his other children, because Joseph was born to him in his old age. Therefore, one day Jacob gave him a special gift--a brightly colored coat.

His brothers of course noticed their father's partiality, and consequently hated Joseph; they could not say a kind word to him.

One night Joseph had a dream and promptly reported the details to his brothers, causing even deeper hatred.

``Listen to this,'' he proudly announced.

``We were out in the field binding sheaves, and my sheaf stood up, and your sheaves all gathered around it and bowed low before it!''

``So you want to be our king, do you?'' his brothers derided. In addition, they hated him both for the dream and for his cocky attitude.

Then he had another dream and told it to his brothers. ``Listen to my latest dream,'' he boasted. ``The sun, moon, and eleven stars bowed low before me!''

This time he told his father as well as his brothers; but his father rebuked him. ``What is this?'' he asked. ``Shall I indeed, and your mother and brothers come and bow before you?''

His brothers were fit to be tied concerning this affair, but his father gave it quite a bit of thought and wondered what it all meant.

One day Joseph's brothers took their father's flocks to Shechem to graze them there.

A few days later Israel called for Joseph, and told him, "Your brothers are over in Shechem grazing the flocks. Go and see how they are getting along, and how it is with the flocks, and bring me word." ``Very good," Joseph replied. So he traveled to Shechem from his home at Hebron Valley.

A man noticed him wandering in the fields. ``Who are you looking for?" he asked.

``For my brothers and their flocks," Joseph replied. ``Have you seen them?"

``Yes," the man told him, ``they are no longer here. I heard your brothers say they were going to Dothan." So Joseph followed them to Dothan and found them there.

But when they saw him coming, recognizing him in the distance, they decided to kill him!

``Here comes that master-dreamer," they exclaimed. ``Come on, let's kill him and toss him into a well and tell father that a wild animal has eaten him. Then we'll see what will become of all his dreams!"

But Reuben hoped to spare Joseph's life. ``Let's not kill him," he said; ``we'll shed no blood--let's throw him alive into this well here; that way he'll die without our touching him!" (Reuben was planning to get him out later and return him to his father.)

So when Joseph got there, they pulled off his brightly-colored robe,

and threw him into an empty well--there was no water in it.

Then they sat down for supper. Suddenly they noticed a string of camels coming towards them in the distance, probably Ishmaelite traders who were taking gum, spices, and herbs from Gilead to Egypt.

``Look there,'' Judah said to the others. ``Here come some Ishmaelites. Let's sell Joseph to them! Why kill him and have a guilty conscience? Let's not be responsible for his death, for, after all, he is our brother!'' And his brothers agreed.

So when the traders came by, his brothers pulled Joseph out of the well and sold him to them for twenty pieces of silver, and they took him along to Egypt.

Some time later, Reuben (who was away when the traders came by) returned to get Joseph out of the well. When Joseph wasn't there, he ripped at his clothes in anguish and frustration.

``The child is gone; and I, where shall I go now?'' he wept to his brothers.

Then the brothers killed a goat and spattered its blood on Joseph's coat,

and took the coat to their father and asked him to identify it. ``We found this in the field,'' they told him. ``Is it Joseph's coat or not?''

Their father recognized it at once. ``Yes,'' he sobbed, ``it is my son's coat. A wild animal has eaten him. Joseph is without doubt torn in pieces.''

Then Israel tore his garments and put on sackcloth and mourned for his son in deepest mourning for many weeks.

His family all tried to comfort him, but it was no use. ``I will die in mourning for my son," he would say, and then break down and cry.

Meanwhile, in Egypt, the traders sold Joseph to Potiphar, an officer of the Pharaoh--the king of Egypt. Potiphar was captain of the palace guard, the chief executioner. (The Living Bible)

This was a terrible thing for Joseph's brothers to do to Joseph and to the rest of the family, but the story does not stop here. Potiphar's wife accuses Joseph of attempted rape and Joseph goes to prison. Joseph spends two years in prison; he helps his cell mates and moves up in rank of prisoners. A high-ranking prisoner is still a prisoner. Those he helped forgot Joseph. None of this would have happened to Joseph if his brothers had not turned against him. All of this was his brothers fault. He had years to build bitterness; instead, he built a life, and became the highest-ranking official in Egypt second only to Pharaoh. How would God have been able to use Joseph if he had become bitter and unforgiving? I think that Joseph would have died a slave in an Egyptian prison. In all of his trials Joseph learned to see God at work in his life. He saw that God was in control of his destiny. Joseph learned to forgive.

Genesis 50: 17-21

17. So shall ye say unto Joseph, Forgive, I pray thee now, the trespass of thy brethren, and their sin; for they did unto thee evil: and now, we pray thee, forgive the trespass of the servants of the God of thy father. And Joseph wept when they spake unto him.

18. And his brethren also went and fell down before his face; and they said, Behold, we be thy servants.

19. And Joseph said unto them, Fear not: for am I in the place of God?

20. But as for you, ye thought evil against me; but God meant it unto good, to bring to pass, as it is this day, to save much people alive.

21. Now therefore fear ye not: I will nourish you, and your little ones. And he comforted them, and spake kindly unto them.

Joseph not only forgave but also was able to show kindness to his brothers and take care of them.

Forgiveness offers freedom to worship and fellowship with God unhindered by the past and all of its misfortunes.

To teach that you should learn to forgive, along with the benefits of forgiveness and not teach *how* to learn to forgive, would be something that I would need forgiveness for.

Learning to forgive:

First, we need to know the forgiveness of Jesus

Colossians 3:13. Forbearing one another, and forgiving one another, if any man have a quarrel against any: even as Christ forgave you, so also do ye.

None of this information would be of any use if you do not know Jesus as your personal Lord and Savior. To know how to forgive you need to be forgiven. Once you experience the love of Jesus, and that love fills your heart you can learn to love others. When you learn how to love with the love of Christ, you can see people through the eyes of Christ and have compassion on them, making it easier to forgive. The first step to learning to forgive is to be filled with the love of Christ.

The second step is you have to choose to forgive. Corrie Ten Boom, who spent years in a concentration camp being tortured by Nazi guards, came face to face with one of her tormentors in a church service that she was to minister. The former Nazi had become a Christian and was attending the church that Sunday. The man approached Corrie Ten Boom and asks for her forgiveness. He reached out his hand to her and she felt resistance, but when she reached out her hand to him, she felt a surge from the Holy Spirit flow through her and a Divine act of forgiveness took place. Corrie Ten Boom acted before feeling. Because of the action, forgiveness took place in her heart then the feeling was there. A lot of times, God expects some action from us and he then brings about His works. The children of Israel marched, before the walls of Jericho fell down. The march came before the victory. Any time you step out in faith to do a Godly thing, God will do a divine thing.

Ephesians 4

31. Let all bitterness, and wrath, and anger, and clamour, and evil speaking, be put away from you, with all malice:

32. And be ye kind one to another, tenderhearted, forgiving one another, even as God for Christ's sake hath forgiven you.

The third step is to think of good things, the Bible tells us to think on things that are good and beautiful. Every time you think of your hurt or something reminds you of the pain you have suffered, stop letting your mind linger there and purposefully think on something good.

This may be hard in the beginning but with almost everything you do, it gets easier with a little practice.

There was once a man who had hurt me and my family pretty bad. At that time, I thought that the best way to forgive someone was to never be around him or her. This philosophy was not working for me. Everyday, I would work out on a kick bag pretending that this man had provoked me to defend my family. I got some good work outs, and psychologists would say that this was a healthy outlet for my anger. One day a Pastor stopped by to ask me to come and help out in his church. Guess who else was attending that church as the minister of education and did the preliminaries at the start of the service. The workouts had not helped. Being around him and seeing the good that he was doing in the church and letting my mind be filled with the good things soon started to crowd out the bad thoughts and we were able to work together until he left the church to pursue a ministry elsewhere. Be kind and tenderhearted to one another. Doing that helped me to get passed the hurt better than the workouts. My body still needs the workouts but my heart became healthy the day I could forgive.

Sometimes you simply need to say it *"I forgive you"* Sometimes you may have to say it a lot. This is the forth step. Confessing it before you feel it may be a lot like the second step but sometimes saying it helps you to accept it in your heart. Sometimes you have to confess to receive. If you hear it you start to believe it. If you say it, you hear it, if you say it enough you accept it, and in accepting it, you forgive in your heart.

Now back to the first thought. "What if it was my daughter and not the business lady's?" I hope and pray that I will never have to answer it. I hope that the grace of God would be on me in such a way that I would be able to follow the steps to forgiveness, because my girl would need someone to help her laugh.

Do not give up on God. Do not give in to your anger, or hurt. Don't shoot the horse.

Chapter 9

Behind the slow driver

Have you ever wondered why the slow driver is always in front? I do not suffer from road rage but I do from time to time get frustrated with some of the things that happen on the road. I used to think that my dark red car was invisible. Every time that I would go somewhere someone would pull out in front of me, AND THEN DRIVE SLOW! I could not figure out why they would be in such a hurry that they would risk their lives by pulling out in front of someone then slowing down. Then it dawned on me, it is not about being in a hurry it is about being in front. People do not want to be second or third, but in front. Another thing that amazes me is this thing that I call the "red prep". The "red prep" is when a driver approaches a green light and rides their brakes preparing for the light to turn red, but the light does not turn red, it turns yellow, and the second it does they take off and make it under the light leaving you, caught by the red light. I know that I am the only one that thinks like this, but these things bother me.

My problem is not bad drivers but little patience; it is not them but me.

World Book dictionary's definition of patience is

> *willingness to put up with waiting, pain, or anything that annoys, troubles, or hurts; calm endurance without complaining or losing self-control*

When we can learn patience then waiting on God will not be a difficult task, we know that He will show up on time and work everything out.

> *Hebrews 6:12. That ye be not slothful, but followers of them who through faith and patience inherit the promises.*

Many people have gone on a quest to discover the keys to experiencing the promises of God, not realizing that the promises of God belong to us because God made them for us. God is a good God, who wants what is best for His children. If you have accepted His son as Lord and Savior then the promises are yours because you are a joint heir with Jesus. People have great faith for the promises but little patience. The Bible tells us it is through faith and patience that we receive his promises. We live in an instant world, or so a lot of people think. We are so used to getting things instantly we believe that God works within our instant world. Take a closer look at instant, is it instant? Not really. You think that you can go to the pantry while the water is heating, take out the box of "instant potatoes" and pour them into the boiling water and suddenly you have mashed potatoes. You don't think about the hours that a farmer spends preparing the soil, planting the potatoes, patiently waiting for them to grow, digging them up, sending them to the factory, where they are cooked and processed, boxed and shipped to the stores. How long does this process take? I do not know, but I do know that it is not instantly. Sometimes when we pray there has to be a process before we see the answer to the prayer. Paul tells us in 1st Corinthians 15:6 *he was seen of above five hundred brethren at once; of whom the greater part remain unto this present, but some are fallen asleep.* If more than five hundred people saw Jesus after the resurrection, why were there only one hundred twenty in the upper room? Just before the ascension, Jesus told those who were with him to tarry in Jerusalem until they received the promise of the Holy Spirit. They had to wait for ten days before the Spirit came. My question is how many of the five hundred knew of the promise of the Spirit? How many lost patience and went home? If you have faith but no patience, you can miss out on some great promises in the Bible.

How can a person learn patience? There is bad news in that question.

James 1:3. Knowing this, that the trying of your faith worketh patience.

Someone once said that if you pray for patience that you will go through trials. When we are faced with trials our patience is often tested.. It would be better to practice patience with the little things in life than to have to go through trials to learn it. Just image how easy life would have been for the children of Israel when they were crossing the wilderness if they had practiced patience instead of complaining about everything. Patience would have shown them that God was taking care of them, and they had no need to worry. Patience would have built their faith. Patience would have shortened their trip, and when they reached the promise land they would have seen that God came through for them. They would have realized, through God, that they would be able to take the land He promised them. Why? Because it is through faith and patience that we inherit the promises of God. I have learned that if you do not learn from the trials you face, you get another chance. I pray for God to make me smarter so I can learn things the first time. But if I do not have to go through a trial to learn something that is a good thing, and patience is something that we can learn without trials. Say a prayer, or listen to music while at the stop light instead of counting how many cars in front of you have their left turn single on. Pay attention to your driving instead of wonder when the driver in front of you is going to turn off that blinker.

One of my favorite Bible stories is the story of Noah and the Ark. Noah showed great patience when building the ark, God told Noah that He was going to flood the earth and destroy all flesh, but Noah found grace in the sight of the Lord. Noah is told by God that it is going to rain, up until this point it had not rained before, so the revelation of rain was revealed to Noah alone, since he was the only one in the world that was considered righteous he was most likely the only one that could hear from God, and the only one that had a concept of what rain was. Noah started to build the ark, which was not an over the night job. Noah worked for one hundred and twenty years on the ark. I believe that during that one hundred and twenty years Noah warned the people of the coming flood. I can see it in my minds eye, people calling Noah that crazy old man who thought water was going to fall from the sky. Noah saw no converts during that one hundred and twenty years. God told Noah to enter the ark because it was going to rain in seven days; it is at this point that my imagination gets somewhat free. I can see in my minds eye the people standing outside of the ark and yelling at Noah "hey Noah I don't see any water falling yet, you been in there seven days now, how long you going to hang on to this fantasy". " Hey Noah, you need to come out and see the sky, it's turning black, and it's getting cooler, hey man you ought to see this." About this time as the taunter looks up at the dark clouds and a large drop of water hit him square in the forehead. Then the bottom falls out of the clouds. As the sheets of rain fall and the water starts to rise, the jokes stop. When the water rises and pours into their houses, the ark starts to float. People swim to the Ark and beat against the sides but there is nothing Noah can do, God had closed the door. Noah waited for one hundred and twenty years for God to fulfill His word, and then seven days closed up in the ark. He waits, patiently. Then he hears the rain beating against the sides of the ark, then waves crashing against the hull, the ark shifts then floats, it rains for forty days and nights then another one hundred and fifty days. Noah had a birthday while in the ark; he was six hundred years old when he entered the ark and six hundred one, one month and twenty-seven days when he left the ark. Maybe it was his patience plus his faith that made him righteous enough to escape the judgment of God.

Luke 21: 19. In your patience possess ye your souls.

There is one other person that we need to consider, this man had a great relationship with God, if fact he was called the friend of God. Abraham was given a promise from God and even though the was a great man of God he failed in this area. When God promised Abraham a child it looked like an impossibility, after waiting for some years for the promise to come to pass, Abraham and Sarah lost patience. They took it upon themselves to make the promise happen, and Abraham had a child with Sarah's servant. God fulfilled His promise through Sara and the descendants of Abraham have not gotten along through all of history. Someone once said that the only thing that we learn from history is that we do not learn from history. However, the Bible is more than history, it is the living word full of examples that we can follow and learn from, there are good example to follow and bad examples not to follow, there are mistakes to learn from, and decisions to be considered. The best example for patience would be God himself. The Bible uses the word longsuffering where God is concerned.

> *Paslms 86:15. But thou, O Lord, art a God full of compassion, and gracious, longsuffering, and plenteous in mercy and truth.*

> *1st Timothy 1:16. Howbeit for this cause I obtained mercy, that in me first Jesus Christ might shew forth all longsuffering, for a pattern to them which should hereafter believe on him to life everlasting.*

> *2nd Peter 3:9. The Lord is not slack concerning his promise, as some men count slackness; but is longsuffering to us-ward, not willing that any should perish but that all should come to repentance.*

Thank God for His patience toward us.

You come to a stop sign and you can see forever both ways and the driver in front of you is just sitting there doing what ever people do at stop signs instead of checking both ways and if clear proceeding with caution, just remember how patient God is with you.

If you do not learn patience then we learn stress, and stress affects out health. So the question, is are you going to be patient or be a patient.

Chapter 10

We all have shoes

The Sharing Thrift Store is an unusual one, to get there you have to go down Experience Express Way and take the first service exit to emotion drive, it's the first building on the left. What is so unusual about the store is the shoe department, it is the largest of its kind, and some of the shoes are well worn with scuffmarks and holes in the soles. There are some shoes that look new, maybe only a mile of wear. Some look like they should have been discarded and others are broken in, but they all are used and have covered a little distance. What makes this store unusual, is not the fact that they have a lot of shoes, but the shoes themselves. If you put on a pair, you feel the experience of the original owners.

Joe Average went into the store one day, after getting off the expressway by accident. Joe was looking for work, or employment which ever he could find, the only problem he had was his lack of experience. His life took a dramatic change when he started trying on shoes. The pair of old work boots on the bottom shelf looked well worn but might be just what he needed when he found a job. Joe slipped the boots on and they were a perfect fit. He paid for the boots and went home, his job hunting finished for the day. The next morning Joe got up and his hands were swollen and hard to close. He was a little slow getting up because of the aching in his back, but when he went down for breakfast, he felt pride in the stiffness. When he saw his family at the table, Joe's wife smiled, she sure looked good standing there in a cotton robe with uncombed hair. The children poked fun at each other and Joe knew in his heart that soreness of muscles and stiffness of his joints was a small price to pay for the well being of those he loved so dearly. Today Joe was going to find some kind of work and provide for his family. His children would go to college and his wife would have a better home. For some crazy reason all he felt he needed was that old pair of work boots. Joe went back to the Sharing Thrift Store and found another pair of shoes, and when he tried them on a totally different feeling came over him. Instead of looking for a job, he went to the coffee shop and spent the day reading magazines and sipping coffee. When he got home, his wife asked him "how did the job hunting go today, you seemed so eager this morning." Joe hung his head and told her were he had spent the day. Joe's wife noticed that he did not have the work boots on anymore but a pair of loafers. She realized there was something about the shoes from that particular store, "take those loafers back to the store and get something you can work in"

Imagine how she felt when he came home wearing a pair of sneakers.

What if Joe went back to that store and found on the top shelf in the back a pair of leather sandals that were around two thousand years old. What would happen if a person really could understand what someone felt by walking in his or her shoes? What if they put on the shoes of Jesus? What kind of compassion would they feel toward a sinful world? Would a person be willing to reach out and touch someone with leprosy? Would they show compassion to someone caught in adultery. How would they treat someone that turned their back on them, a friend and companion that claimed they did not even know them? If by putting on the shoes of Jesus you suddenly understood his feelings and purpose, would it have an impact on you? Better yet, would anyone notice a difference in your life? We cannot put on the shoes of Jesus but the Bible tells us, For as many of you as have been baptized into Christ have put on Christ. *(Galatians 3:27)* I would think that putting on Christ would have a greater impact on our lives than wearing his shoes.

When I was the Chaplain at a mission, one of the female residences asked to speak to the group during morning devotion. She stood and told things about her life. She told of abandonment by her parents, of prostitution, and alcohol. When she finished she said that no one understood. That to truly, understand you would have to walk a mile in her shoes. When she finished everyone was silent and waiting for me to respond to this young lady's outburst. I stood and went to the podium, and it occurred to me what to say. I looked at the young lady and said, "We all have shoes, I have not walked your miles in your shoes, but I have walked my miles in my shoes." Everyone's shoes and miles are filled with hurt and disappointments, those experiences shape who we are. The way we react to the experiences is what makes us. I knew two people who's parents were alcoholics. One grew up to rely on alcohol, the other grew up to despise it.. The one who despised alcohol actually became a health fanatic, putting nothing in her body that was harmful, the other became a drunk. We have all walked many miles. I do not need to experience your pain to know pain, and I do not need to go through your disappointments to know disappointment, I have plenty of my own. Because I have experienced hurt, I can relate to your hurts.

"I know what you are going through" is not a good statement of comfort to someone who is experiencing hurt or lost. Even when it is the same situation, the people who experience it are different people, some recover more quickly than others, some are stronger. Just because people experience the same hurt does not mean that they feel the same type of pain. I can reach out to someone who is hurting, not because I know his or her pain, but because I have known my own pain.

The Savior who knew every kind of hurt, great compassion, unbounded love, and unbelievable forgiveness, lives inside all who have invited Him to do so. Jesus did not let the hurt over rule His compassion, love, or forgiveness. These characteristics of Christ in us is what helps us help others Even when we do not fully understand their pain we feel compassion for them in their trials, love them through their valleys, and forgive them when they are not understanding toward you. Do not give up on people; they can be rescued from any circumstance they fall into.

Chapter 11

Why a manger

And she brought forth her firstborn son, and wrapped him in swaddling clothes, and laid him in a manger; because there was no room for them in the inn.
Luke 2:7

For we have not an high priest which cannot be touched with the feeling of our infirmities; but was in all points tempted like as we are, yet without sin.
Hebrews 4:15

What did Jesus get for Christmas? It was not gold, frankincense and myrrh. That came possibly two years later when Joseph and Mary were living in a house. On the very first Christmas, there were no presents for Jesus, to unwrap but instead, he was wrapped in swaddling clothes and laid in a feeding trough. There were no David and Goliath dolls to play with and no chariots going around a little track. There was no tree sparkling with lights with a star on top. There was a star though, shining high in the heavens above a blanket of others. There were no carolers standing outside the stable singing Joy to the World, but out on a hillside angels sang to shepherds about a savior. On that first Christmas day Jesus got nothing and was not even in his own home but a little stable. When all the children or adults stand and complain about missing out on Christmas Jesus can stand among them and say I understand I have been there.

When Jesus was twelve years old, he got to go with his parents for the first time to the Passover feast in Jerusalem. Jesus went to the temple and got so carried away with the teachers that he did not leave with his parents to go home. Joseph and Mary's perspective was that Jesus had been missing for three days. When they finally found him in the temple, `Son!" his mother said to him. ``Why have you done this to us? Your father and I have been frantic, searching for you everywhere." ``But why did you need to search?" he asked. ``Didn't you realize that I would be here at the Temple, in my Father's House?" (Living Bible)

Jesus knew what he was doing but his parents just did not understand. Is this a new feeling for a young person? I do not think so. All young people, at some time or another, feel that their parents do not understand how they feel or what they are going through. When they all stand together Jesus will stand among them and say, "I understand, I've been there." There is one important note to make, Jesus was the only young person who actually did know more than his parents, and the Bible tells us that Jesus was subject unto them.

What happened to Joseph? He was there when Jesus was born, and he was there when Jesus was twelve, at the temple. When Jesus entered His public ministry, Joseph is not mentioned. Neither is he mentioned when Mary, Jesus and His disciples went to the wedding at Cana. Many Bible teachers believe that Joseph died when Jesus was still young. We know that Jesus lost his cousin by a tragic death early in his ministry. Jesus knows what it feels like to lose a loved one to death. He knows the void and the loneliness, the hurting. Jesus can stand with all those who have suffered losing a family member and say I know how you feel, I have been there.

Next comes the wilderness temptation of Jesus. Some seem to think that this was the only temptation of Jesus, but I believe since he was "in all points tempted as we are" that he faced temptations all of his life. He felt hunger in the wilderness, there were times when as a baby he felt hunger. I imagine that Mary even had diapers to change. The whole purpose for Him to be born and raised as a human was to know the hearts and troubles of humankind.

The Wilderness Temptation

> *And when the tempter came to him, he said, If thou be the Son of God, command that these stones be made bread. Matthew 4:3*

Turning stones to bread because He was hungry was not the temptation. The temptation was to misuse His powers for personal gain, to satisfy the lust of the body.

I have a problem with people who use their power or influence for personal gain. I do not believe that a minister should use pulpit time to influence political votes. Even if you really believe in a candidate and what they stand for, you have to know that the true answer for the problems a person or society may face is Jesus. Why take time set aside to proclaim Jesus and His saving power to promote a man who is running for a political office? While we need Godly men in political offices, they do not need to be promoted from the pulpit. A pastor should not use his influence to sway the vote of his flock. Some use their popularity and influence to raise money.

> *Acts 1: 8. But ye shall receive power, after that the Holy Ghost is come upon you: and ye shall be witnesses unto me both in Jerusalem, and in all Judaea, and in Samaria, and unto the uttermost part of the earth.*

God gives us gifts from the Holy Spirit so we can be witnesses of Jesus. The gift of singing is not given to bring glory to the singer but to God, to point people to the Savior. Does this mean that a singer can not sing anything but Christian songs? God also gifts for our enjoyment.

> *Thou dost show me the path of life; in thy presence there is fulness of joy, in thy right hand are pleasures for evermore. A Prayer of David. (Psalms 16:9 RSV)*

Our pleasure and enjoyments should always be clean and decent. The singer that is tempted to sing about unwholesome things for prosperity sake but chooses instead, to keep their talent clean, honors God.

Jesus was hungry, if He had not been, then using His power to turn stones into bread would not have been a temptation.

1st John 2 :16 tells us about the different kinds of temptation.

> *For all that is in the world, the lust of the flesh, and the lust of the eyes, and the pride of life, is not of the Father, but is of the world.*

The temptation of satisfying His hunger by abusing His power would be giving in to the lust of the flesh.

And when the woman saw that the tree was good for food, and that it was pleasant to the eyes, and a tree to be desired to make one wise, she took of the fruit thereof, and did eat, and gave also unto her husband with her; and he did eat. Genesis 3:6

There is a parallel between the temptation of Eve and the temptation of Christ. The first, being the lust of the flesh. She saw that the tree was good for food. Jesus was tempted to create food, she gave in, Jesus did not.

Jim came to the mission, where I was serving as the chaplain, seeking a place to stay. Jim had been an air traffic controller but lost everything that was precious to him because of alcohol. He poured his life out just like he poured booze out of a bottle and as he swallowed his drink, his career, and family were also swallowed into non-existence. I had coached his daughter in softball that same year, so I felt a connection to him. I gave him a book that dealt with times of crisis in the life of Jesus, hoping it would encourage him through his troubled time. A few days later, he gave the book back and told me that he enjoyed it but Jesus knew before hand what the out come would be. I tried to explain that if we accept Jesus as our personal Lord and Savior that He would work out all our problems, but you have to trust Him. Jim eventually accepted the Savior and one night slipped into eternity to be with Jesus. One thing that Jim had a hard time understanding was that Jesus did understand his hurts and disappointments. Jesus may have known the final outcome of His mission, but we can also know ours. The Bible tells us that all things work together for our good if we love God and are called according to his purpose. What is the purpose of

God? The Bible also tells us that God is not willing that any should perish but that all would come to repentance. God's purpose is simple, to have a relationship with you. Accepting Jesus as your personal Savior enters you into a relationship with God. God takes care of His own; it is a good thing to know that the Creator of the universe is taking care of you. He knows what is best and will fulfill it in our lives when we learn to give in to His will. We may not know the exact outcome of trials in our lives but we can know that God works out what is best for us, even if we do not understand what or why things are happening the way they are. We also know that this life is not final but just the start of our eternal journey. Take it with God.

The second wilderness temptation

> *5 Then the devil taketh him up into the holy city, and setteth him on a pinnacle of the temple, 6 And saith unto him, If thou be the Son of God, cast thyself down: for it is written, He shall give his angels charge concerning thee: and in their hands they shall bear thee up, lest at any time thou dash thy foot against a stone. Matthew 4:5&6*

Was the temple the only high place that Satan could tempt Jesus to cast Himself from? I do not think so, there had to be other tall places. The Bible tells of mountains, cliffs, high walls and many other high places, but the temple was safe ground, this was His Fathers House. Do you think that a person can be tempted to sin at Church? We have all heard the stories of affairs between the preacher and the piano player. Christians have done more to hurt christianity than anyone or anything else. The problem is not being tempted but giving in to it. If Satan can enter the presence of God like he did in Job you better believe that he is working in the

Church. So where can you be safe? It is not in Church it is "in Christ" that we find strength to resist the devil.

This temptation is actually the third one listed in First John, "the pride of life". Look at me, how special I am, look at how successful I am, even look at how blessed I am. Eve saw that the tree would make her wise. Jesus could show how special He was. Eve gave in to the temptation, and Jesus did not.

The third wilderness temptation.

> *8. Again, the devil taketh him up into an exceeding high mountain, and sheweth him all the kingdoms of the world, and the glory of them;*
>
> *9. And saith unto him, All these things will I give thee, if thou wilt fall down and worship me. Matthew 4:8&9*

This would be the lust of the eyes. Eve saw that the tree was pleasant to the eyes, and Jesus was shown all the glories of the kingdoms of the world. Have you ever wondered what Jesus saw when He was shown the glories of the kingdoms? Remember that He came from Heaven. I believe that He saw things that appealed to the flesh. Jesus was hungry and weak, He may have seen banquet tables filled with food, and He may have seen young maidens dancing around in their sensual attire. That was the temptation that cost John the Baptist his head. I do not know exactly what He saw but I do know that it was pleasing to the eyes, and Satan knows what is pleasing to our eyes. The price was too high for Jesus; He could not and would not betray His Father. Eve gave in to the temptation, Jesus did not. Adam and Eve giving in to the temptation brought condemnation to the world. Jesus, by resisting temptation brought hope and salvation to the world.

Satan had the power to tempt Jesus, and he has the power to tempt us. Jesus had the power to resist and the gives that power to us, using that power, is up to us.

Luke's account of the wilderness temptation ends with this verse.

And when the devil had ended all the temptation, he departed from him for a season. Luke 4:13

Did you see that last phrase? Satan departed from Him for a season. I think that may mean that Satan came back to try again. Satan will not give up on you, but neither will Jesus. Hang in there with Jesus, He will never leave you, He is a very loving and forgiving Savior. He has been where you are and will take you to where you need to be. Just don't shoot the horse.

Chapter 12

Stories Told to Me

For he shall give his angels charge over thee, to keep thee in all thy ways. Psalms 31:11

The State Trooper

"Randy, I've come back to the Lord." That is how a friend started his extraordinary tale one morning when I met him on the sidewalk outside the business were he worked. Jimmy had gone out of town to try to reconcile with his estranged wife.

"I was sitting there in her living room and everything seemed to be going great, she was telling me that I should move out there were she lives, and I thought that we were going to get back together". Jimmy looked at me and then shook his head. "Then she got up and started getting herself ready for a date she had that night". He continued, "I couldn't take it, so I got up and left." Jimmy got quite for a moment then looked at me and said, "As I was driving back I was thinking about what had happened and not paying much attention to the speed limit." Jimmy had a very fast mustang, "and I asked God 'God do you love me anymore, do you even care?' about that time a state trooper pulled out with his lights flashing and pulled me over, I thought this is all I need." " The trooper came over to the car and said 'Sir do you know how fast you were going' I told him I did not, He took my driver license looked at it, handed it back to me and said, ' Jimmy, I'm not going to ticket you, I just want you to know that God loves you and that He cares'. Looking at me, he just shook his head and said, " I just clung to the steering wheel and cried like a baby."

The Lady in White

I was sitting at a table outside a snack bar one day when a friend walked by and invited me to a revival at his church. He was telling me about the revival when he ask me if I had heard about his daughter. I told him that I had not, this is what he told me.

"I got the call late one Thursday night that there had been an accident and we needed to get down to the hospital as quick as possible. When we got to the hospital we learned that my daughter had veered off of the road and struck a telephone pole. She hit the pole so hard that it snapped in half. The doctor came out and told us that she was going to be fine and that she was a very lucky young lady. A police officer came up and wanted to know what happened to the passenger? When they arrived on the scene there were two people in the car and when they got the driver side door opened they pulled only my daughter out and the other person was missing. I knew that she was not supposed to have any passengers so I did not know what to tell the officer. When the Doctor told us that we could see our daughter we hurried in to the room to fine her looking a little bruised but beautiful all the same.

When the opportunity arose, I asked about the passenger. She said," there wasn't anyone riding with me" then she thought for a minute and said, "I do remember someone in the car right after I wrecked, a beautiful woman dressed all in white and she would touch my face and tell me everything was going to be okay, and every time she touched me the hurting would stop. I don't know where she went."

My friend smiled and looked at me and said, "Randy there was an Angel in the car with my baby and it saved her life".

The Alabama Fan

This story appeared in the local newspaper. I tell it in my own words because it happened several months ago, but it sticks in my mind.

A couple wanted to go to the Alabama - Auburn game, these are the rival colleges in the state, and in Alabama, you are born a fan of one of these colleges. Getting tickets to this game late in the season is almost impossible. This couple decided to advertise in the paper for tickets. Someone gave them tickets to the game but they had to sit on the Auburn side of the stadium, and they were Alabama fans. People were wondering why Alabama fans were sitting on the Auburn side, in a sea of orange and blue were two red and white jackets. During the game, someone yelled for help, sitting two rows behind the Alabama fans a man had a heart attack and was not breathing. The Alabama fan who had been a medic in the army knew what to do and went in to action. Performing CPR, he kept the man alive until the rescue team arrived and took over. The man survived because an army medic just happen to get free tickets for the wrong side of the stadium, and in the midst of thousands just happen to be sitting two seats in front of someone about to die. Was it all just coincidence or a loving God working things out for one of his children?

My Story

I was young, in the fifth grade and living in a trailer park about a mile from the school. I would ride my bicycle to school each day. One day I chose not to cross the street at the school crossing but go down the street and cross where the entrance to the trailer park was. I thought I looked both ways that day and can't imagine where the car came from, but when I rode out into the street, I was right in front of an oncoming car. There was nothing the driver could do, he was to close to swerve or stop but he tried. I heard the horn and the brakes but I was out there and there was nothing I could do. Suddenly the front wheel of the bicycle was lifted off the road and the bike was turned ninety degrees and sat down next to the curb. The car came to a stop yards down the street and the man shouted out the window, "did I hit you?" I told him that he did not, he was scared and I was scared but everything was fine. I went home, put my books up, went down in the woods, and prayed. I believe that an angel picked up the front of my bicycle and moved me from the front of the oncoming car, saving my life, why, I do not know. I do know that God loves me, and one day will use me to help others.

Chapter 13

Regaining your wow

The school child watches wide eyed while the egg begins to shake a little. A crack appears in the top of the shell, next, a hole, then a tiny bird pushes its head up through the hole in the shell and the only word that can escape the child's mouth is "wow".

One of the definitions of wow in the World Book dictionary is to overwhelm with delight or amazement. God gives us something every day that would overwhelm us with delight or amazement, if we would take the time to notice it.

When I was riding a bike for exercise in the mornings, I noticed that there were a lot of wild flowers growing on the side of the road. My favorite was morning glories, they would blanket the side of the road and come in many colors, some would be pink and others blue, some were a lavender color and some a deep dark purple. I hardly noticed them growing on the side of the road while driving sixty miles an hour in a car; but when I slowed down to a bicycle ride I recognized the beautiful gift God had given me. When was the last time you were so amazed by God's creation that you had to stop and just take it all in? Most of the time we are to busy to take that time, and we miss the wonderful things that God graces us with.

There are some great sights in the world that people will take vacation time to visit and experience. I have never seen the Grand Canyon or the northern lights, nor have I experienced the green hills of Ireland or the shores of Hawaii, but I have been to Pretty Place. Pretty Place is close to the border of South Carolina and North Carolina. To reach it you have to drive up the mountain and when you reach the top, you come to a chapel. Once inside the chapel, you find that it has no back,, and you are looking out across the Carolina mountains. It is one of the prettiest sights you will ever see. While I was there a devout Christian woman looked out across the scenery and tears filled her eyes because of the beauty and the grace of God. The view is so grand that you cannot help but to feel the presence of God, maybe that is why they built a chapel on that mountain top. It is good to get away and experience such grand sights as Pretty Place, but God gives us little gifts every day that would amaze you if you would take the time to view them. Have you ever just sat and closed your eyes and listened to the birds sing, or watched the sun set on the beach? I am told that if you are on the beach at sunrise and it is very clear that at the right moment you will see a flash of emerald green on the horizon. I have never witnessed the emerald flash I've only read about it, but I have been in the mountains on cold winter days and awoken to trees that appeared to be made of crystal adorned with diamond leaves. I have been there during the fall when the leaves start changing colors and it looks like God opened a treasure chest and poured it out across the mountains, the hills flowing with emeralds, rubies and gold.

Do you take the time to notice the many gifts that God gives you every day? Do you hear the music of the wind and the artistry of the sunset or the reflection of the stars on the calm lake in the middle of the night? We hear sermons on the beauty of heaven, the pearly gates, streets of gold, and Crystal Sea, and we look forward to experiencing the glories of heaven, but there are glories on earth. After all, God created the earth just as He did heaven.

> *Isaiah 61:3. To appoint unto them that mourn in Zion, to give unto them beauty for ashes, the oil of joy for mourning, the garment of praise for the spirit of heaviness; that they might be called trees of righteousness, the planting of the Lord, that he might be glorified.*

> *1st Chronicles 29: 11. Thine, O Lord is the greatness, and the power, and the glory, and the victory, and the majesty: for all that is in the heaven and in the earth is thine; thine is the kingdom, O Lord, and thou art exalted as head above all.*

> *Psalms 96:6. Honour and majesty are before him: strength and beauty are in his sanctuary.*

Have you ever had your feelings hurt because you did something special for someone and they did not even notice your effort? Children often leave a room with their heads hung low because a parent did not appreciate a good grade on a paper or a good report card. A school drawing is tossed in a box instead of hung on the refrigerator door. Why does God create so many splendors in our everyday world if they are not for us to enjoy? You may say that God is the creator and it is just in Him to create. Do not forget that He has an entire universe to work His artistry in, places where absolutely no one would see His handiwork. Who's to say that those places are not filled with incredible scenes? I believe that He creates here on Earth for our pleasure, and if we would start to appreciate His works that He would find great pleasure in us, and wow might become a regular part of our vocabulary.

On the southeastern coast of Sweden in 1886, a pastor was visiting a beautiful countryside when there was a sudden thunderstorm. The wind blew violently, the lightning flashed constantly with thunder rumbling, and as suddenly as the storm appeared, it blew out and the sun emerged shining bright and clear. The birds started to sing in the calm of the day. Pastor Carl Boberg was struck with such awe that he bowed and started to worship the Creator. He later wrote a poem that after some time was turned into a song titled "How Great Thou Art" Have you ever experienced an act in nature that inspired you to worship your maker? I have. I once worked at an airfield that was one of the highest elevations in the area. One evening, a strong storm blew in and out in a matter of a short time. The storm left a cloud formation in the western sky that became a spectacular sight as the sun started to set. The colors that spread across the sky made one of the most beautiful sunsets I had ever seen. I was parked facing the west enjoying the scenery when someone banged on the window. I looked around and there was one of my co- workers pointing to the east and said, "Look". I turned around to see three rainbows stacked on top of each other. I had never seen anything like that before. The sunset in front of me and the rainbows behind me, I did not know which way to look, but I knew what to say, "WOW"

It is good to realize that God is still active in this world, that we are not alone. God is with us and if He cares enough about us to put morning glories on the side of the road He will put other things in our lives to make our journey, one full of joy and abundance.

The Bible tells us that He sees the sparrow, knows the number of hairs that are on our heads, that He loves us maybe that is the reason that He gives us sunsets and rainbows.

Psalms 8

1. O Lord our God, the majesty and glory of your name fills all the earth and overflows the heavens.

2. You have taught the little children to praise you perfectly. May their example shame and silence your enemies!

3. When I look up into the night skies and see the work of your fingers--the moon and the stars you have made--

4. I cannot understand how you can bother with mere puny man, to pay any attention to him!

5. And yet you have made him only a little lower than the angels, and placed a crown of glory and honor upon his head.

6. You have put him in charge of everything you made; everything is put under his authority:

7. all sheep and oxen, and wild animals too,

8. the birds and fish, and all the life in the sea.

9. O Jehovah, our Lord, the majesty and glory of your name fills the earth.

(The Living Bible)

Chapter 14

Resurrection of the Heart

Jesus told Mary that He was the resurrection and the life; of course, He was speaking of the resurrection of the dead but sometimes more than the body dies.

People experience the death of many kinds of things in their lives. Has your hope died, how about your love, or faith? Has someone killed your spirit or ambition? Has your enthusiasm been smothered, your compassion stomped out? Does your attitude stink like it has died? There are a lot of things that we go through that can kill part of the soul. John 10:10 tells us that the thief comes to kill, steal and destroy. It is not just the body he is after but also the heart. He is constantly attacking the heart. He is the master of the heart attack.

What do you do when you come under one of these attacks on the heard? What do you do when your soul suffers a death blow? There is a Savior who can heal the wounded heart. He can resurrect the dead attributes of the heart and give abundant life to the lifeless soul. If you have had a funeral of the heart in one or more of these areas, you are not in bad company. Some of our Bible hero's suffered the same loss.

Let us look at some of them and maybe we can see how we can experience a resurrection of the heart.

First, let us look at lost hope in the story of Mary Magdalene in John chapter 20.

> *1. The first day of the week cometh Mary Magdalene early, when it was yet dark, unto the sepulchre, and seeth the stone taken away from the sepulchre.*
>
> *2. Then she runneth, and cometh to Simon Peter, and to the other disciple, whom Jesus loved, and saith unto them, They have taken away the Lord out of the sepulchre, and we know not where they have laid him.*
>
> *3. Peter therefore went forth, and that other disciple, and came to the sepulchre.*
>
> *4. So they ran both together: and the other disciple did outrun Peter, and came first to the sepulchre.*
>
> *5. And he stooping down, and looking in, saw the linen clothes lying; yet went he not in.*
>
> *6. Then cometh Simon Peter following him, and went into the sepulchre, and seeth the linen clothes lie,*
>
> *7. And the napkin, that was about his head, not lying with the linen clothes, but wrapped together in a place by itself.*

8. Then went in also that other disciple, which came first to the sepulchre, and he saw, and believed.

9. For as yet they knew not the scripture, that he must rise again from the dead.

10. Then the disciples went away again unto their own home.

11. But Mary stood without at the sepulchre weeping: and as she wept, she stooped down, and looked into the sepulchre,

12. And seeth two angels in white sitting, the one at the head, and the other at the feet, where the body of Jesus had lain.

13. And they say unto her, Woman, why weepest thou? She saith unto them, Because they have taken away my Lord, and I know not where they have laid him.

14. And when she had thus said, she turned herself back, and saw Jesus standing, and knew not that it was Jesus.

15. Jesus saith unto her, Woman, why weepest thou? whom seekest thou? She, supposing him to be the gardener, saith unto him, Sir, if thou have borne him hence, tell me where thou hast laid him, and I will take him away.

16. Jesus saith unto her, Mary. She turned herself, and saith unto him, Rabboni; which is to say, Master.

17. Jesus saith unto her, Touch me not; for I am not yet ascended to my Father: but go to my brethren, and say unto them, I ascend unto my Father, and your Father; and to my God, and your God.

18. Mary Magdalene came and told the disciples that she had seen the Lord, and that he had spoken these things unto her.

Who was Mary Magdalene? According to Mark 16:9 Jesus had cast seven devils out of her and some believe that she was the sinner that washed the feet of Jesus with her tears and dried them with her hair. She was at the cross when all of the disciples but John were elsewhere. Her devotion to Jesus was so strong that some have even speculated that they were married. I believe that Jesus will only have one bride and that is the church, but Mary's devotion to Jesus is evident.

When Jesus died on the cross, all was lost to Mary. The one who showed her kindness and acceptance was gone. Her future was gone, her hope was lost. She went to the tomb that Sunday morning to be near her savior, and take care of his body, only to find that it too was gone. She ran to tell the disciples then returned to the garden where Jesus was buried. When the Savior appeared to her, she was so sure that He is gone she did not recognize Him.

Jesus said "Mary" and she knew who he was.

2. he that entereth in by the door is the shepherd of the sheep.

3. To him the porter openeth; and the sheep hear his voice: and he calleth his own sheep by name, and leadeth them out.

4. And when he putteth forth his own sheep, he goeth before them, and the sheep follow him: for they know his voice.

When He called her by name, she recognized His voice and Hope was resurrected.

If you have lost hope, go to the place where you last heard the Savior and listen for the voice, you will recognize it when you hear your name. You will feel the voice deep down in your heart, because the heart will be filled with His love.

What happened to Mary after the resurrection? She continued to serve the Lord, she is considered to be a saint and there is a church named for her in Russia. Tradition holds that she even made her way to a banquet being given by Emperor Tiberius Caesar. When she met him she produced an egg and proclaimed, "Christ is risen" the egg being a symbol of new life. The Emperor laughed and said that the chances of Christ being raised from the dead were as unlikely as the egg turning red. Before he finished speaking the egg turned bright red in her hand, and she continued proclaiming the Gospel to the entire royal house. This started the tradition of dyeing Easter eggs. It is believed that Mary, after spreading the Gospel, went to Ephesus to live with Mary the mother of Jesus and died at the age of seventy-two.

Sometimes people may lose their faith, Elijah did. Elijah was one of the greatest prophets of the Old Testament. Through the power of God he raised the dead, held back the rain and defeated the prophets of Baal by calling down fire from heaven. Then things took a bad turn when Jezebel threatened him.

1st Kings 19

1. And Ahab told Jezebel all that Elijah had done, and withal how he had slain all the prophets with the sword.

2. Then Jezebel sent a messenger unto Elijah, saying, So let the gods do to me, and more also, if I make not thy life as the life of one of them by to morrow about this time.

3. And when he saw that, he arose, and went for his life, and came to Beersheba, which belongeth to Judah, and left his servant there.

4. But he himself went a day's journey into the wilderness, and came and sat down under a juniper tree: and he requested for himself that he might die; and said, it is enough; now, O Lord, take away my life; for I am not better than my fathers.

Elijah had done a lot for the Lord and after having outrun Ahab's chariot he was very tired, then receiving the news from Jezebel that she was going to kill him, he lost faith.

Have you ever done your best for the Lord only to come under attack? You work until you are worn out. You're just tired, and don't know where to go or what to do, maybe you even feel that God has let you down and you are all alone. What do you do?

Then he lay down and slept beneath the broom bush. But as he was sleeping, an angel touched him and told him to get up and eat!

He looked around and saw some bread baking on hot stones, and a jar of water! So he ate and drank and lay down again.

Then the angel of the Lord came again and touched him and said, ``Get up and eat some more, for there is a long journey ahead of you."

So he got up and ate and drank, and the food gave him enough strength to travel forty days and forty nights to Mount Horeb, the mountain of God,

where he lived in a cave.But the Lord said to him, ``What are you doing here, Elijah?"

He replied, ``I have worked very hard for the Lord God of the heavens; but the people of Israel have broken their covenant with you and torn down your altars and killed your prophets, and only I am left; and now they are trying to kill me, too."

"o out and stand before me on the mountain," the Lord told him. And as Elijah stood there the Lord passed by, and a mighty windstorm hit the mountain; it was such a terrible blast that the rocks were torn loose, but the Lord was not in the wind. After the wind, there was an earthquake, but the Lord was not in the earthquake.

And after the earthquake, there was a fire, but the Lord was not in the fire. And after the fire, there was the sound of a gentle whisper.

when Elijah heard it, he wrapped his face in his scarf and went out and stood at the entrance of the cave. And a voice said, ``Why are you here, Elijah?''

He replied again, ``I have been working very hard for the Lord God of the armies of heaven, but the people have broken their covenant and have torn down your altars; they have killed every one of your prophets except me; and now they are trying to kill me, too.''

Then the Lord told him, ``Go back by the desert road to Damascus, and when you arrive, anoint Hazael to be king of Syria. Then anoint Jehu (son of Nimshi) to be king of Israel, and anoint Elisha (the son of Shaphat of Abel-meholah) to replace you as my prophet. Anyone who escapes from Hazael shall be killed by Jehu, and those who escape Jehu shall be killed by Elisha! And incidentally, there are 7,000 men in Israel who have never bowed to Baal nor kissed him!'' (The Living Bible)

What we read in this story first, is that even when we are down, God is still there and providing for us. We do not have to see Him to know that He is there. He is always with us. Remember that God loves you like a parent loves a child, and will never leave or forsake you. David said that it did not matter where he went God would be there. When Elijah was at his lowest God sent angels to minister to him, did he recognize them as angels? I do not know, but I do know that God sends ministers to help his children; the ministers may be angels or people being led by the Spirit. I do know that it is a good feeling to be the one God uses to help someone when they are down. The Bible tells us that God is no respecter of persons, what He did for one He will do for all. In the chapter "Stories told to me", I relate several stories where angels were sent to help people in our present day. God is still working on our behalf.

The nourishment that God gave Elijah, gave him strength to travel forty days to Mount Horeb. Mount Horeb was one of the mountains that were in the same range as Sinai, it was in a wilderness place. A lot of times, people would go to the wilderness to have an encounter with their God, a place where they could be alone with God. It was there that God spoke to Elijah, "what are you doing here Elijah". Elijah whined " I've done everything I could do for the Lord and the only place it got me was alone, I'm the only one left to serve the Lord, why don't you go ahead and let me die.

God told Elijah to get out of the cave. Has God ever told you to get out of your comfort zone? To do something that you would not naturally do, like speak to a stranger, or pray for someone in a wheelchair, or perhaps teach a Sunday school class.

When Elijah stepped out of the cave, there was a mighty wind that shook the mountain, God was not in the wind, then came an earthquake. God was not there either, then came a mighty fire, God did not show up in the fire. Where was God? In the heart of Elijah, close enough for him to hear a soft whisper of the Father. That is where we will find God, right where He is supposed to be, in our hearts. Sometimes we just need to learn to listen to the voice of God. If we will listen, He will speak, it may not be in something spectacular. It may be but a soft whisper in the heart. That whisper is more powerful than any act of man or nature.

Then God told Elijah," by the way, there are seven thousand who have not bowed to Baal, you were never alone."

Getting alone with God, hearing his voice, and finding out that He was always in control gave Elijah's faith a boost. Then God told Elijah to get up and get busy.

Lost your faith? Get alone with God, and listen for a whisper.

Has your love died? You may want to read about the woman at the well in John chapter 4.

> *4. He had to go through Samaria on the way,*
>
> *5. and around noon as he approached the village of Sychar, he came to Jacob's Well, located on the parcel of ground Jacob gave to his son Joseph. Jesus was tired from the long walk in the hot sun and sat wearily beside the well.*
>
> *7. Soon a Samaritan woman came to draw water, and Jesus asked her for a drink.*
>
> *8. He was alone at the time as his disciples had gone into the village to buy some food.*
>
> *9. The woman was surprised that a Jew would ask a ``despised Samaritan" for anything--usually they wouldn't even speak to them!--and she remarked about this to Jesus.*
>
> *10. He replied, ``If you only knew what a wonderful gift God has for you, and who I am, you would ask me for some living water!"*

11. ``But you don't have a rope or a bucket,'' she said, ``and this is a very deep well! Where would you get this living water?

12. And besides, are you greater than our ancestor Jacob? How can you offer better water than this which he and his sons and cattle enjoyed?''

13. Jesus replied that people soon became thirsty again after drinking this water.

14. ``But the water I give them,'' he said, ``becomes a perpetual spring within them, watering them forever with eternal life.''

15. ``Please, sir,'' the woman said, ``give me some of that water! Then I'll never be thirsty again and won't have to make this long trip out here every day.''

16. ``Go and get your husband,'' Jesus told her.

17. ``But I'm not married,'' the woman replied.``All too true!'' Jesus said. ``For you have had five husbands, and you aren't even married to the man you're living with now.''

19. ``Sir,'' the woman said, ``you must be a prophet.

20. But say, tell me, why is it that you Jews insist that Jerusalem is the only place of worship, while we Samaritans claim it is here [at Mount Gerizim], where our ancestors worshiped?''

21. Jesus replied, ``The time is coming, ma'am, when we will no longer be concerned about whether to

worship the Father here or in Jerusalem. For it's not where we worship that counts, but how we worship--is our worship spiritual and real? Do we have the Holy Spirit's help? For God is Spirit, and we must have his help to worship as we should. The Father wants this kind of worship from us. But you Samaritans know so little about him, worshiping blindly, while we Jews know all about him, for salvation comes to the world through the Jews."

25. The woman said, ``Well, at least I know that the Messiah will come--the one they call Christ--and when he does, he will explain everything to us."

26. Then Jesus told her, ``I am the Messiah!" (Living Bible)

The story of the woman at the well is a long one but it is so important. It was not a common thing for a Jew to go through Samaria to travel from Judea to Galilee; instead, they would cross the Jordan River and then cross back over to Galilee. The Samaritans were a mixed race and considered impure, and the Jews had no dealings with them. The Bible telling us that Jesus must need to go through Samaria is not because that was the only road to take. There was a meeting to take place between a hurting woman and a loving Savior. It was the common practice for people to go the well in the early morning or late in the evening. To go in the middle of the day was a rare thing to do, reserved for the outcast of society. I imagine she could feel the eyes of the people watching her as she made her way down the street to go to the well. With her head bowed with shame and embarrassment because of a lifestyle that was a reproach to the community, she makes her way to the well. She had no idea of the encounter that was destined to take place. God going out of his way in search for fallen man.

I think that the woman's heart had lost its ability to love. A person who has had five spouses and now a "live in" no doubt has had damage to the heart. What has happened to her ability to love, to really love others? It was taken from her heart one piece at a time, and with each piece a hole is left in the heart until the heart is empty.

Have you ever felt like the woman at the well? Have so many pieces been taken from your heart that is has been left empty? You feel like you have nothing left to offer, you have no desire to offer anything even if you had it. Love has abandoned you. What do you do? What did the woman do? Nothing.

Jesus made it his mission to meet the woman, to step outside tradition into taboo and change the life of a hurting woman. What would Jesus be willing to do to heal your hurts, to reach out to you, where would He go to meet you? He has already gone there, He stepped out of Heaven to the cross. On the cross He took your hurt, take him into your heart, let him fill it completely.

When the woman approached the well she had no idea what was going to happen, she may not have been surprised to see Jesus sitting at the well, but was shocked that He would speak to her. Jews had no dealings with the Samaritans, men did not speak to women in public, and a rabbi defiantly did not speak to a woman. God was the first to view men and women as equals, when He said that He was no respecter of persons He meant it, male or female, He loves them same. He spoke to the woman and told her that there was something that would fill her heart and her life and make everything

OK. If you accept Jesus into your heart, He will fill you with a river of life. Go to the Savior, sit and talk with Him. Jesus sent the disciples away because the woman needed to spend some time alone with the Son of God. If you will make time to spend with the Savior He will talk with you. Keep a receptive heart, and whatever damage may be there will be healed when you are alone with Jesus.

After spending time with Jesus, the woman being filled with that river of life went to the city and shared with the people. The outcast was accepted and the people went to meet this Christ. The disciples went into town for food and came back with food; the woman went to town with news of the Messiah and came back with the people. The lost love was replaced with the love of Jesus and that love was shared with a whole town.

We have only covered three of the eight attributes that I mentioned at the start of this chapter, the other five are all tied up in the character of Jonah. We studied Jonah in an earlier chapter, but we need to take one more look at this broken hearted prophet.

Jonah was ordered to go to Nineveh, an evil city that took sport in torture and idol worship. Jonah did not want to go; in fact, he ran from God and took a short cut to Nineveh by way of a whale. Jonah preached that the city was facing destruction and the city from the King down repented, so did God. The city was spared and Jonah was disappointed. He felt that God had let him down.

Jonah chapter four tells Jonah's disposition

> *1. But it displeased Jonah exceedingly, and he was very angry.*

2. And he prayed unto the Lord, and said, I pray thee, O Lord, was not this my saying, when I was yet in my country? Therefore I fled before unto Tarshish: for I knew that thou art a gracious God, and merciful, slow to anger, and of great kindness, and repentest thee of the evil.

3. Therefore now, O Lord, take, I beseech thee, my life from me; for it is better for me to die than to live.

4. Then said the Lord, Doest thou well to be angry 5. So Jonah went out of the city, and sat on the east side of the city, and there made him a booth, and sat under it in the shadow, till he might see what would become of the city.

6. And the Lord God prepared a gourd, and made it to come up over Jonah, that it might be a shadow over his head, to deliver him from his grief. So Jonah was exceeding glad of the gourd.

7. But God prepared a worm when the morning rose the next day, and it smote the gourd that it withered.

8. And it came to pass, when the sun did arise, that God prepared a vehement east wind; and the sun beat upon the head of Jonah, that he fainted, and wished in himself to die, and said, It is better for me to die than to live.

9. And God said to Jonah, Doest thou well to be angry for the gourd? And he said, I do well to be angry, even unto death.

> *10. Then said the Lord, Thou hast had pity on the gourd, for the which thou hast not laboured, neither madest it grow; which came up in a night, and perished in a night:*
>
> *11. And should not I spare Nineveh, that great city, wherein are more than sixscore thousand persons that cannot discern between their right hand and their left hand; and also much cattle?*

Jonah had definitely lost his compassion, his attitude was stinking pretty badly, under that vine, he had no enthusiasm, it seemed like his very spirit had died. God was prepared for Jonah's condition from the start. He prepared the whale, the gourd, the worm, and the heat. Nothing can happen to you that will catch God unprepared; He knows the future before it happens. Remember that God cares for you and will not let anything happen to you that you cannot bear, with any test, He will make a way of escape.

How did God rescue Jonah's heart? He let Jonah see things from His perspective. Sometimes when we do not understand why things happen if we seek, God He will let us see things from His perspective, and maybe we will gain insight of how things really work together for our good.

In every situation, that I mentioned in this chapter the solution was to get alone with God and let Him deal with your damaged heart. Revelation 3:20 tells us that Jesus stands at our hearts door and knocks, if we open the door Jesus will come in and fellowship with you. The problem that many people have is that they will only open the door part way, just enough for Jesus to get his foot in the door. If you will open the door of your heart wide open, then Jesus will come in fully and fill your heart. For the troubled, the Prince of

Peace will come in, for the mourning the Father of Comfort will come in, for the hurting the Healer will come in, for the bound the Deliverer will come in, for the lost the Savior will come in. What ever your need, Jesus is the answer. Open your heart all the way and He will come in all the way. Do not give in to your problem, give in to the Savior.

Chapter 15

Mysteries and Secrets

In the last chapter we talked about opening the door of your heart. With all the things we covered in this book, there is only one answer and that is Jesus, but you have to give him a chance. There are some mysteries and secrets in the Bible we need to learn that I hope will build your relationship with the Savior. The first is the mystery of the third temple or the dwelling place of God.

The first temple. King Solomon built the first temple after David had collected all the materials for the building,

> `By hard work I have collected several billion dollars worth of gold bullion, millions in silver, and so much iron and bronze that I haven't even weighed it; I have also gathered timber and stone for the walls. This is at least a beginning, something with which to start.
>
> And you have many skilled stonemasons and carpenters and craftsmen of every kind.

They are expert gold and silver smiths and bronze and iron workers. So get to work, and may the Lord be with you!" (The Living Bible 1st Chronicles 22:14-16)

God would not let David build the Temple because he was a man of war, so Solomon picked up the task in his fathers place. Solomon built a magnificent temple for the Lord, and when he had the dedication service for the temple, God showed up and moved in.

10. And it came to pass, when the priests were come out of the holy place, that the cloud filled the house of the Lord,

11. So that the priests could not stand to minister because of the cloud: for the glory of the Lord had filled the house of the Lord. (1st Kings 8)

God moved in. God was in the Temple like He was on Mount Sinai and it is interesting to note, the temple was built on Mount Moriah where God had proclaimed He would prepare a sacrifice for the sin of the people. The temple stood as a grand reminder that God was in the mist of Israel. Nebuchadnezzar finally destroyed the temple, and many of its treasures were carried off to Babylon.

The second temple. Under the leadership of Zerubbable and the high priest Jeshua, when the people returned from captivity they started to restore their ancient worship by rebuilding the temple. Twenty years after returning from captivity the temple was completed and ready for consecration. This temple had some important things missing like the ark, the holy oil, and sacred fire, as well as the tables of stone along with the pot of manna and Aaron's rod. These things were carried away to Babylon, it was later that they were restored to the temple by King Cyrus. The temple stood for around five hundred years when Herod the Great became king of Judea. During which time the temple had suffered damaged from decay and assaults from enemy armies. Herod remodeled the temple to gain favor with the Jews and it stood until the Romans took the city of Jerusalem by storm and the soldiers set fire to it totally destroying it in 70 A.D. and it has never been rebuilt.

The third temple. There will be a temple built in Jerusalem during the last days and the anti-christ will commit the abomination of desolation, polluting the Sanctuary as told by Daniel in Daniel 11:31. Many people believe this to be the third temple. I believe the third temple is the body of Christ.

> *Jesus answered and said unto them, Destroy this temple, and in three days I will raise it up. John 2: 19*

The temple is the dwelling place of God and Jesus was God incarnate in the flesh then His body is the temple, and if you have accepted Jesus as your Lord and Savior then you are a part of the body of Christ, and the temple of God.

> *Know ye not that ye are the temple of God, and that the Spirit of God dwelleth in you? If any man defile the temple of God, him shall God destroy; for the temple of God is holy, which temple ye are. 1st Corinthians 3: 16-17*

Here is where it gets really interesting. The Doors of the second temple were made of iron and brass and from the trees of Lebanon. They were so huge that it took twenty men to open or close the doors. There is a reference concerning the doors of the temple in the Jewish writings that make up their law called the Talmud.

> *"Forty years before the destruction of the temple the lot did not come up in the right hand, nor did the crimson stripe become white, nor did the westernmost light burn: and the doors of the heikhal (the Holy Place of the Temple) opened of their own accord, until Rabbi Yochanon ben Zakkai rebuked them. He said to it. "O heikhal, heikhal, why do you alarm yourself? I know full well that you are destine to be destroyed, for Zechariah ben Iddo has already prophesied concerning you ' Open thy doors, O Lebanon, that the fire may devour the cedars' (Zech. 11:1).' Talmud Bavli, Yoma 39b*

What makes this reference from the Talmud so amazing, is that it is forty years before the destruction of the temple. The temple was destroyed in A.D. 70 making the doors to open by themselves in A.D. 30 the year Jesus was crucified in Jerusalem. This incident is not only recorded in the Talmud, but also in the works of Josephus the first century historian that wrote the history of the Jews.

> *Moreover, the eastern gate of the inner (22) [court of the] temple, which was of brass, and vastly heavy, and had been with difficulty shut by twenty men, and rested upon a basis armed with iron, and had bolts fastened very deep into the firm floor, which was there made of one entire stone, was seen to be opened of its own accord about the sixth hour of the night. Josephus; The War of the Jews 6.5.3*

There are two historical records that the temple doors opened by themselves, the Talmud puts it the same year that Jesus died, I believe it was the same day. The temple was the dwelling place of God, but when Jesus took our sin upon himself, a new temple was created, and that temple is the believer. The door opened because the temple of the body of Christ was being destroyed, not Herod's temple. I think the doors opened because GOD MOVED OUT of the old temple and moved into the new temple. Are you the temple of God? There is one door that stands between you and God, and God will not open it, you have to, it is the door of your heart.

Revelation 3: 20. Behold, I stand at the door, and knock: if any man hear my voice, and open the door, I will come in to him, and will sup with him, and he with me.

Open the door all the way; He will come in all the way. He chooses you to live in, not great temples, fancy cathedrals, or even a galaxy filled with stars. He longs to live in you, and He knocks and calls out to you. Open the door today and live life abundantly. Is there anything that can keep you from hearing the voice of Jesus calling to you? We did an illustration with some young people to show how it is sometimes hard to hear God. We lined all the youth around the walls of the youth center and blindfolded one of the young men, then hid an object in the room and some of the teenagers were to give instructions to the blindfolded young man as to where the object was hidden, but the rest of the teenagers were to give false directions. The young man heard too many directions and did not know which way to go. Take all the teenagers out of the room and let one give directions and he finds the object.

Do you ever feel like there is too much going on in your head and life to hear anything coming from the heart? Sometimes you have to get alone with God. God had to get Moses into the wilderness to speak to him. Adam and Eve were in a garden alone with God and we read were Jesus had to go to a solitary place to pray. That is what the Bible means when it tells us to go to a closet. God is not telling you to sit under your hanging coats with the light out, He is saying get alone, anywhere it would be just you and Him, a stream running behind your house, maybe a field with wild flowers and singing birds, or on the side of a lake or beach, it does not matter where or how it does matters that you get alone with Him. Sometimes after you pray and worship you need to be quiet and listen. What will He tell you? It might be "stand still and see the salvation of the Lord," like He told Moses. He might say "open the door of your heart and let him in all the way, into every corner and secret place of your life." He might say "hang on, joy is coming in the morning," He may and most likely would say, "I love you my child". Whatever He says you need to hear it, so listen!

The Secret Place of the Stairs

> *Song of Solomon 2:14 O my dove, that art in the clefts of the rock, in the secret places of the stairs, let me see thy countenance, let me hear thy voice; for sweet is thy voice, and thy countenance is comely.*

The Hebrew name for this book is "Song of Songs" meaning this is the best of all other songs. The Song of Solomon is an allegorical poem showing the love that exists between Jesus and the believer illustrated by the relationship between the bridegroom and the bride. Ezekiel 16 describes Israel as a woman that God took and loved. Revelation 19:7 tells us,

Let us be glad and rejoice, and give honour to him: for the marriage of the Lamb is come, and his wife hath made herself ready.

The custom of the Hebrew wedding is an interesting one. When a man and a woman were engaged, they were considered to be married, even though there had not been an actual wedding ceremony yet. That is why Joseph was considering divorcing Mary when he found out she was expecting. They had no physical relations yet, but were considered married because she was promised to him. When they were engaged, the man would leave a gift with the bride and go away to build their home. When the home was finished and the time of the wedding was here, the groom would go for his bride. When the wedding party saw him coming, they would announce his arrival "behold the bridegroom cometh" and blow trumpets. The last trumpet would announce the start of the wedding. After the wedding feast the groom would take his bride to their new home and they would "tabernacle together." Does this sound like anything you have heard before? Let me give you a clue.

1. Let not your heart be troubled: ye believe in God, believe also in me.

2. In my Father's house are many mansions: if it were not so, I would have told you. I go to prepare a place for you.

3. And if I go and prepare a place for you, I will come again, and receive you unto myself; that where I am, there ye may be also. John 14

What God wants is intimacy with us; the kind you see in newlyweds. The kind that tears their hearts out when they cannot be together, and leaves a void to be filled only when they are in each other's arms again. The kind that makes you feel like it would be impossible to live without them. God wants that with us. Husbands if you received the kind of attention from your wife that you give God, how would you feel? Wives, if your husbands treated you like you treat God, would you be married today? Did you once have that "got to have you love for your spouses" and somehow lost it? It happened to the Church. The Church at Ephesus is commended for their love for all saints in Paul's letter to them. (Ephesians 1:15) Forty years latter Jesus tells the Church at Ephesus He had something against them because they had lost their first love. (Revelation 2:4) Jesus tells them to return to their first love. Christians we need to return to the kind of romantic love affair with God that we had with our spouses when we first got married. How do you go back there? We go to the secret place of the stairs. You will not be the first to go there, Abraham went there, so did Moses and David, Paul and John. What is the secret place of the stairs? In the castle, there were secret stairs leading to the bedroom chamber of the groom. Only the bride was to know the location of the stairs. What is it to us? The way, the privilege to access the presence of God. How can we find the secret place of the stairs?

The first step on the stairway is delight.

> *Psalms 34:4. Delight thyself also in the Lord: and he shall give thee the desires of thine heart.*

Delight is something that gives great pleasure and joy. Do you take delight in your children? When you were first married, did you take delight in your spouse? David delighted in the Lord; he said he was glad when they said to him "let us go unto the house of the Lord". Where did David learn this delight? I think it may have started in a pasture. He was alone with a harp, green fields, and quite streams. The sheep would graze and David would contemplate the grace, mercy, and goodness of God. If we would take time to read the psalms of David we would see that with the troubles he faced at times, he always had hope in God. Then we would also see times of simple worship, and delight in his Lord. David knew how to delight in God; we too need to learn this.

The second step on the stairway is desire.

> *Psalms 42:1. As the hart panteth after the water brooks, so panteth my soul after thee, O God.*
>
> *2. My soul thirsteth for God, for the living God: when shall I come and appear before God?*

Newlyweds have a desire for each other, not just a physical desire but also an emotional one. My wife will sometimes call our daughter just to hear her voice on the answering machine. God has that kind of desire for us, and we should for Him. Moses had it. After spending forty day in the presence of God on Mount Sinai, Moses wanted more. He pleaded With God to see Him. God placed him in the cleft of a rock and passed by to let Moses see His backside as He passed by. I think the cleft of the rock may have been Jesus himself and to see God we need to hide in the cleft of the rock of ages.

Paul had that desire. Paul had a close encounter with Jesus on the road to Damascus, receiving a special revelation of the savior that changed everything about Paul. Even with this experience under his belt, Paul wanted more.

> *Philippians 3:10. That I may know him, and the power of his resurrection, and the fellowship of his sufferings, being made conformable unto his death;*

To have a desire to know Jesus is to have a craving that cannot be satisfied. To always want more. To have a desire for Jesus will get you to the third step on the stairway.

Dependence. Today people want independence. "I do not need anyone or anything, I'm self efficient". When you do not need anyone, you only end up lonely. To need God is wisdom. To realize you need God is the starting point of wisdom.

Delight, desire and dependence, the secret place of the stairs. Do you take delight in God? Do you desire Him? Are you dependent on Him? Where will the stairs take you? To an intimate relationship with the creator of the universe, a savior that died for you and longs to know you and you Him.

The Secret of God

> *Job 29:4. As I was in the days of my youth, when the secret of God was upon my tabernacle;*

The Hebrew word for secret here is cowd, which means a session, by implication intimacy. Intimacy is to have a close personal relationship. The Hebrew word for tabernacle here is 'ohel, which means covering, (dwelling) (place), home, tabernacle, tent. (*Strong's Hebrew Dictionary*) This tells me that Job could remember a time when he had an intimate relationship with God and this relationship was upon his home. Is this possible today? Yes it is. If it were not possible, God would be a respecter of persons.

Then Peter opened his mouth, and said, Of a truth I perceive that God is no respecter of persons: (Acts 10:34)

God does not put one person over another, and what he will do for one He will do for any. So how did Job reach the place of the secret of God being upon his home? *But thou art holy, O thou that inhabitest the praises of Israel. (Psalms 22:3)* Inhabitest = dwell, in other words God lives in the praises of His people. Would you like God to live with you like He did Job? One way for that to happen is to live a life of praise.

Psalms 117

1. Praise the Lord, all nations everywhere. Praise him, all the peoples of the earth.

2. For he loves us very dearly, and his truth endures. Praise the Lord.

Another way is to live a life of gratitude.

Chapter 16

Thanks a Lot

Queen Juliana of the Netherlands had to flee her home and country when Nazi Germany occupied her country. She was a princess at the time she went to live in Ottawa, Canada. She lived in a normal house, shopped in local stores, and her children went to the local school. Canadian troops played a major role in the liberation of the Netherlands, allowing the Princess to return home. After returning home, Princess Juliana sent 100,000 tulip bulbs to Ottawa in gratitude for the hospitality the Canadian people had shown her and for their efforts in the freeing of her country. This was the start of an annual Tulip Festival in Ottawa, Canada. Juliana then sent 15,000 tulip bulbs for the Festival every year until her daughter took over the throne in 1980, and then the government of the Netherlands started sending tulip bulbs annually for the Festival. Ottawa, after receiving the tulip bulbs for a few years, became quite an attraction and pictures of the tulip beds started showing up in newspapers. Different types of events were added to annual bloom of tulips, and in 1953 Canada their first Tulip Festival, and soon the Tulip Festival grew to an awesome display of over two million flowers.

Don't Shoot the Horse

The Canadian Tulip Festival has become the largest festival of its kind in the world. Thousands of people from everywhere travel to experience the beauty of the Tulip Festival; their pleasure and enjoyment all come from the gratitude of one extraordinary woman.

Aesop said that, "Gratitude is the sign of noble souls" and a French Proverb tells us that, "Gratitude is the memory of the heart." An unknown author tells us "Gratitude consist of being more aware of what you have, than what you don't." **Gratitude** is a positive emotion, which involves a feeling of emotional indebtedness towards another person; often accompanied by a desire to thank them or to reciprocate for a favour they have done for you. (*Wikipedia, the free encyclopedia*)

Gratitude is not always an act but a lifestyle. We say thank you to the server when they fill our cup out of politeness, but when we realize how hard it would be to finish our meal without something to drink, we say thank you out of appreciation for the drink and the server.

The Pilgrims made seven times more graves than huts. No Americans have been more impoverished than these who, nevertheless, set aside a day of thanksgiving. --H.U. Westermayer

There are health benefits to living a life of gratitude. There have been studies to show that a life of gratitude can promote physical and emotional well-being, and it can be helpful in dealing with stress as well as improve a person's ability to interact with others. Grateful people seem to have more energy and fewer complaints than the ungrateful.

We live in such a self-absorbed world that it has been suggested that only one of ten people experience the positive emotion of gratitude. Living in a generation of many negative emotions that rip apart our families, hearts and lives, rob us of health, peace and happiness, requires the need to practice positive emotions to counter act the effects of anger, hurt, loneliness and depression. Gratitude is not only a positive emotion but will help us discover other positive emotions that will enhance our lives.

During World War II, the Germans had to defeat the Royal Air Force to be able to cross the English Channel and invade England. The German Air Force bombed British ships and ports, and began nightly raids on London. The Royal Air Force was greatly out numbered but took to the air to defend England and finally defeated the German Air Force. Winston Churchill expressed the nation's gratitude to the brave pilots with these words, "Never in the field of human conflict was so much owed by so many to so few."

When you think of stories like Queen Juliana and the British Royal Air Force and the gratitude that they experience and felt, you cannot help but think about what Jesus did for us and continues to do on a daily basis. We can echo the words of Winston Churchill and say, "never in the field of human existence has so much been owed to one, Jesus Christ". I mentioned earlier that I love sunsets, and when I see the bright colors in the sky, I know it is a special gift from God because there are people like me who love sunsets and God loves us. I love to hear the birds singing in the morning and enjoy the fresh morning air, a gift from God. There are millions of gifts that God gives to us but none can compare to the gift of His Son for our salvation. Because of the gift of salvation, we can enjoy all the other gifts that come to us day by day. Christians should be some of the most emotionally sound people in the world, but we are not. Maybe we should practice the art of gratitude and show a world what it means to be happy.

Let us take a look at what the Bible tells us about gratitude.

> *In every thing give thanks: for this is the will of God in Christ Jesus concerning you. 1st Thessalonians 5:18.*

Some people point out that this verse tells you to give thanks in all things and not for all things but…..

> *Ephesians 5:20 Giving thanks always **for** all things unto God and the Father in the name of our Lord Jesus Christ;*

Giving thanks in all things is easer than giving thanks for all things. Even when you are going through a very hard time, you can thank God for so many other things that are good in your life. It is a more difficult thing to thank God for the very hard times. How can we do it?

> *And we know that all things work together for good to them that love God, to them who are the called according to his purpose. Romans 8:28*

If we love God and put Him first in our lives, we can have faith that all things, even the bad things, will work together for our good. God loves us, wants good things for us, and will work things out for our good. When we truly believe this simple principle, we can thank God even for the hard times in our lives.

> *let us offer the sacrifice of praise to God continually, that is, the fruit of our lips giving thanks to his name.* Hebrews 13:15

Sometimes giving thanks may be a sacrifice, but for our own benefit, is a sacrifice worth giving.

There was a song we sang in church when I was growing up entitled "Count Your Blessings." Some of the words went like this, "count your blessing, name them one by one, count your blessings see what God has done". When we are going through some of those hard times, we need to remember the faithfulness of God and remember all the blessings He has given us in the past and believe the blessings have not stopped, but will come again soon.

> *For thou, LORD, wilt bless the righteous; with favour wilt thou compass him as with a shield.* Psalms 5:12

> *The LORD will give strength unto his people; the LORD will bless his people with peace.*
>
> Psalms 29:11

> *O taste and see that the LORD is good: blessed is the man that trusteth in him.* Psalms 34:8

> *Then shall the earth yield her increase; and God, even our own God, shall bless us.* Psalms 67:6

There are too many verses on the blessings of God to mention them all, but I hope you get the picture with these verses. The blessings will come when we learn to simply be thankful to God for all His blessings.

There is a story in Luke we need to take a look at Luke 17: 11-19

> And it came to pass, as he went to Jerusalem, that he passed through the midst of Samaria and Galilee. [12] And as he entered into a certain village, there met him ten men that were lepers, which stood afar off: [13] And they lifted up their voices, and said, Jesus, Master, have mercy on us. [14] And when he saw them, he said unto them, Go shew yourselves unto the priests. And it came to pass, that, as they went, they were cleansed. [15] And one of them, when he saw that he was healed, turned back, and with a loud voice glorified God, [16] And fell down on his face at his feet, giving him thanks: and he was a Samaritan. [17] And Jesus answering said, Were there not ten cleansed? but where are the nine? [18] There are not found that returned to give glory to God, save this stranger. [19] And he said unto him, Arise, go thy way: thy faith hath made thee whole.

The first thing I notice is that it was important to Jesus that the one man came back to give thanks. The Bible tells us we are to be Christ like and this is one area where we achieve it. Everyone wants to be appreciated for the favors we give others, but living in an unthankful world, we like Jesus may experience gratitude only ten percent of the time. The people that show gratitude to us are more likely to receive favors from us more often than those who are not grateful.

The Bible tells us the one that returned was a Samaritan, the others were likely Jews. The Samaritans and the Jews were very prejudice toward each another. Leprosy broke down the walls of prejudice and the men stood and lifted there voices together. Conflict can bring the most unlikely people into unity, because they have their hardship in common. Why can't people see the positive things in their lives, recognize the same things in the lives of others, and build relationships on them? I am a Christian. That alone gives me something in common with people throughout the country, if we can put aside theological differences and simply enjoy brothers and sisters in the Lord.

Why did the nine not return to give thanks? Were they so excited about their healing that they simply forgot? That makes them look a little bad, but how often do good things happen to us and we forget to give thanks for them.

And thou shalt rejoice in every good thing which the LORD thy God hath given unto thee. Deut. 26:11

It is a good thing to give thanks unto the LORD, and to sing praises unto thy name, O most High: Psalms 92:1

The nine may have been anxious to get their health certificates from the Priest and go home to their families. You can hardly blame them for that. But the one that really stands out to Jesus, is the one that returned. He was still going to go to the Priest and return home to his family, but there was something in his heart needing to fall before the Savor and thank Him, it was gratitude. All ten were healed, but the one with the heart of gratitude I believed lived a happier life because of his attitude.

I have been writing this book on and off for several years, and the first chapters have stories of my wife. During the course of this book, our marriage failed, resulting in divorce. I will not blame my wife or take the blame, only that it happened. I have never been so devastated in my life, the hurt went deep and I feel it will last a long time. It was during this time I started this chapter and to begin with, it was very difficult to continue writing. With head knowledge, I started to write and found something that was very strong and was helping me through my time of heartache. One day while driving to work, I started thanking God for the things I have. I thanked God for my daughter, Erica, who told me I would always be her daddy. I thanked God for my niece, Kellie, who is like my own child; she told me she would always be mine and I would always be her uncle. I thanked God for my parents that are still living and are healthy, who took me in and said they were glad to have me there. I thanked God for the many friends who kept asking about me and praying for me. I thanked God for the sixteen years I had with my wife. I thanked God for His promise that He would work all things together for my good. How I did not see or understand what the future holds, I do not know.

Sometimes ministers will get a word from God, a word to encourage and comfort the hurting and confused. One Sunday a guest speaker was at my church and he was quite

Funny and I was having a good day, so I was not sitting there looking depressed. The Minister finished his sermon and did not give a call for prayer, he just came straight to me and laid his hand on my shoulder and said, "I just want you to know that you have a bright future." Then he said (this is what he really said) "I don't know what kind of do-do you've been through, but you know the faithfulness of God and you have a bright future!" You can believe what you want to about things like this but I believe God saw my breaking heart and wanted to give me hope for the future. God is the God of broken pieces. While there are some things that may not work out the way we hope for them to, there is one thing for certain, God will not leave us or forsake us and will work things out for our good. Some things we have to take in faith, and not shoot the horse.

Chapter 17

The God of Broken Pieces

§

The English Civil War took place between 1642 and 1651 and consisted of three different armed conflicts between the Parliamentarians, those that supported the Parliament, and the Royalist, those that supported the King. During the second conflict the town of Colchester, a walled city with a castle and several churches, was fortified by the Royalist and was laid siege by the Parliamentarians. Standing next to the city wall was St. Mary's Church, a huge cannon was placed on the wall of St. Mary's Church to defend the city. In mid July, a shot from a Parliamentary cannon damaged the wall of St. Mary's Church that supported the cannon and the cannon went crashing to the ground. The cannon was so big that the Royalist soldiers and Calvary could not pick up the cannon and place it on another wall. Near the end of August, with the loss of the cannon, the Royalist had to lay down their arms, open the gates of Colchester, and surrender. The cannon that defended the city of Colchester had a famous name, Humpty Dumpty. Humpty Dumpty did not become an egg until illustrated in Lewis Carroll's story "Through the Looking Glass".

Humpty Dumpty sat on a wall

Humpty Dumpty had a great fall

All the Kings horses and all the Kings men

Could not put Humpty Dumpty together again.

I have a cousin named Duane. If ever there was someone that would have a right to speak to Job it would be Duane. Duane had a happy life. He married his childhood sweetheart, and together they were raising a family in a happy home where everything was going well. Duane and his wife were active in church and loved God with all their hearts. One night Duane's house burned to the ground and they lost everything. They put their lives back together again and went on. Then one day a tragedy shook their lives. Their baby girl, just over two, was killed in a random accident involving a car's electric window. They flew her to the Children's Hospital where she was put on life support but was determined to be brain dead. Her mother held her in her arms when life support was disconnected and she ceased to function; the soul was already with Jesus. This was not the end of the tribulation of Duane, his loving wife became ill and it was discovered she had cancer. The cancer took Duane's wife but not his spirit. Duane had two more children to take care of, and a savior to hold him. Today Duane has two beautiful girls a lovely wife and a nice home. He hung in there with God and put the pieces together again.

Has something happened to make your life fall apart? Have you suffered something so devastating that you feel like your whole world has crumbled? Has circumstances beyond your control shattered your very existence? Have you experienced the humpty dumpty syndrome, that you are broken to pieces and all the kings' men and all the kings' horses cannot put you together again? I have. My life shattering experience was a divorce. Duane's, a lot more. Yours may be more than Duane's or less than mine; whatever it is, it is still shattered.

All the king's men and all the king's horses might possibly be the Minister's and Christian friends that have reached out to you, and while they have been some comfort to you, they cannot put you together again. There are times when your circumstances need special attention, when the king's men and horses fall short. There are times when you need the special attention of the King, and only He can put you together again. Jesus is the King, the God of broken pieces, and when there are pieces missing, He can fill in the voids.

One of the neat things about the Bible is we can read the Whole story. We can see the where lives have fallen apart and we can see where God put them together again. Hang in there and you will experience the rest of the story of your life and witness the God of broken pieces putting it together again.

Let us take a look at one of the broken lives of the Bible; you find a good example in the character of Ruth.

Ruth 1

1. Long ago when judges ruled in Israel, a man named Elimelech, from Bethlehem, left the country because of a famine and moved to the land of Moab. With him were his wife, Naomi, and his two sons, Mahlon and Chilion.

3. During the time of their residence there, Elimelech died and Naomi was left with her two sons.

4. These young men, Mahlon and Chilion, married girls of Moab, Orpah and Ruth. But later, both men died, so that Naomi was left alone, without her husband or sons.

This story starts off going down hill. There is a famine in Israel so Elimelech decided to move from Bethlehem. Bethlehem in the Hebrew language means house of bread. Why was there a famine in the house of bread? Is there a famine in the house of bread today? Are there churches today not feeding their people? Are people moving from church to church trying to find a place to be fed? Sometime it is better to stay and wait for the famine to end than run from it. Elimelech named his two sons Mahlon and Chilion, meaning sickly and the pining one. These young men were doomed from the start. The sons married Moabite women, which was a no-no since the time Balaam advised the King to seduce the Israelite men with the Moabite women and brought the displeasure of God on all of Israel. Elimelech and his two sons die in Moab; they left the house of bread to die in a foreign land. Before they died, they married two Moabite women, Ruth being one of them. Now let us pick up the story from the perspective of Ruth.

How Ruth and Chilion got together is not told in the Bible, only that Ruth became Naomi's daughter-in-law. The Bible does not tell how long they lived in Moab, but it was long enough for them to meet, fall in love and get married, and for Ruth to become so much a part of the family that she wanted to stay a part even after her husband died. It was forbidden in Hebrew law for an Israelite to marry anyone outside their race. It was also forbidden for a Moabite to enter the Sanctuary, so there had to be difficulties in the relationship from the start. It is note worthy to notice they overcame these difficulties and that Ruth is in the linage of Jesus.

Ruth becomes part of Naomi's family and they start to suffer loss and heartbreak.

Ruth's father-in-law, who was the main provider for the family, dies and now the chores fall on Sickly and Pining. Things are not looking up. Sickly dies and all the family's responsibilities fall on Pining. This may have been to much for him because he also dies.

There are now three women left alone. Life was not easy for a woman left alone in this ancient world.

It is no wonder Naomi wanted to leave Moab as she had only suffered during her stay there. It would be better to go home and live with famine, than to stay in the country of her trouble. Naomi urged her two daughters-in-law to go back to their families. Oprah said good-bye, but Ruth would not leave Naomi.

> 16. But Ruth replied, ``Don't make me leave you, for I want to go wherever you go, and to live wherever you live; your people shall be my people, and your God shall be my God;
>
> 17. I want to die where you die, and be buried there. May the Lord do terrible things to me if I allow anything but death to separate us."
>
> 18. And when Naomi saw that Ruth had made up her mind and could not be persuaded otherwise, she stopped urging her.

19. So they both came to Bethlehem and the entire village was stirred by their arrival. ``Is it really Naomi?'' the women asked.

20. But she told them, ``Don't call me Naomi. Call me Mara,'' (Naomi means ``pleasant''; Mara means ``bitter'') ``for Almighty God has dealt me bitter blows.

21. I went out full and the Lord has brought me home empty; why should you call me Naomi when the Lord has turned his back on me and sent such calamity!''

22. (Their return from Moab and arrival in Bethlehem was at the beginning of the barley harvest.) (Living Bible, Chapter 1)

The Bible does not tell us why she would be more willing to go to a foreign land than to return home to be with her family. Some teach that she was very devoted to Naomi, and had been converted to the Israeli faith. There is the possibility also that Ruth's family had disowned her because she had married outside of her people, and she simply had no where else to go.. I do not know her reasoning, only that as a young woman she was uprooted from her home and moved to an unfamiliar land, and there was no provision for them when they arrived at their new home. I remember when I was young, we had to move from north Alabama to south Alabama. I did not want to move, but my father accepted a job in south Alabama. All the things that were home, the house, my room, the yard, the block that I would ride my bicycle around, friends, neighbors and family would be staying and we were leaving. Moving is hard on a child, but I had my mother and father and a brother to go also. Ruth only had Naomi and a great responsibility to take care of her. Ruth's world had completely fallen apart; if you read the story carefully, it is not hard to see God taking care of both Ruth and Naomi. God helped provide for them to the point of placing Ruth in the ancestry of Jesus. I enjoy reading stories of people God rescued and put their lives back together.

Boaz married Ruth, and when he slept with her, the Lord gave her a son.

14. And the women of the city said to Naomi, ``Bless the Lord who has given you this little grandson; may he be famous in Israel.

15. May he restore your youth and take care of you in your old age; for he is the son of your daughter-in-law who loves you so much, and who has been kinder to you than seven sons!"

16. Naomi took care of the baby, and the neighbor women said, ``Now at last Naomi has a son again!" And they named him Obed. He was the father of Jesse and grandfather of King David. (Living Bible, Ruth 4:13-18)

Ruth is not the only one in the Bible that had their world shattered. In fact, I cannot think of anyone who did not have their world fall apart at some point in their lives. Adam and Eve were kicked out of the garden, which changed their lives dramatically. They then lost their first two children, one to murder, the other to exile. Then God started putting their lives back together again. Noah did not lose his immediate family, but what about his brother and sisters and their families. Noah had his whole world literally washed away. He then inherited the whole world.

Abraham had to leave his home when he was a young man, but his father stopped short of making it to the promise.. When Abraham became a man, he had to leave his home again when there was a conflict between him and his nephew. Abraham's nephew, Lot, is kidnapped and Abraham has to launch a rescue. One of the greatest blessings a man could receive in those days was to have a son. Abraham had to wait ninety years for this blessing. Nevertheless, the blessing came.

There is someone else whose world fell apart. Take a look at Job. Let us move Job from the Bible to modern day America and call him Joe, and tell the story using my liberal imagination. Joe could be your neighbor or a member of your church, here is his story.

Joe is a pillar of the community, a leader in the Church, he gives to charity and loves his family and prays for them everyday. Joe has become very successful in business and wants for nothing but to see his whole family in church and serving God.

One day Joe Junior invites all of his brothers and sisters to his house for a special party. It was not a good day to have a party as a severe band of storms was headed their way.

Joe called his children and told them to be careful and he took his wife, Lisa, and headed for the basement to wait out the storms. They waited and listened to the radio for hours, there was news of lightning strikes and a couple of tornados as well as and flash flooding. When morning came and the storms passed, Joe and Lisa climbed the stairs to see if there had been any damage to their home. They stepped out on the porch and were filled with relief to find their home was undamaged. The ringing of the cell phone startled them and as Joe lifted the phone to his ear, his heart sank to his stomach. Lisa moved close to him and held his arm as he answered. The voice on the other end was the manager of the larger of his two stores. "Joe I have some bad news, the store was struck by lightning during the storm and even in the rain it still burned to the ground. Everything was lost. I'm so sorry Joe." Joe said, "Everything will be okay, at least no one was hurt." Joe ended the call only to have the phone ring again, "Hello" Joe answered, "Joe this is Sam from the store in the valley. The store flooded last night and we lost everything, Joe it was all destroyed." "That's okay Sam, at least no one was hurt" Joe replied. Joe was beginning to feel very sick by this time. His whole business had been wiped out in just a few hours. The phone rang again, "what now" Joe thought, he could see the fear in Lisa's eyes as he answered. "Hello," the voice on the other end was grim, "Joe this is Sheriff Owens. You need to come to Joe Junior's house right away." Joe was afraid of what the problem might be, he and Lisa just ran to the car. Joe Junior lived close so it did not take long for the remains of the house to come into view. Fear gripped Joe's heart and Lisa began to cry, but it only got worse as they stopped in front of where the house once stood. There were several police cars, two fire trucks, three rescue vans, and no survivors. All of Joe and Lisa's children were gone. Joe crumbled to the ground with a heart winching wale, Lisa passed out, and it started to rain again.

The Pastor spoke beautiful words at the funeral that Joe did not hear. Friends hugged him and Lisa, and there was lots of food in the dining room, but Joe could not eat. Standing by the graves Joe said, "God is in control and we should give thanks in all things." Lisa gave him a hard unbelieving look, and his friends could not believe the strength Joe displayed. But Joe knew the only way he would survive would be through God. There was no explanation that could satisfy

Don't Shoot the Horse

Joe and Lisa. While Joe hung on to his faith, Lisa started to grow bitter with God for allowing something like this to happen, and with Joe for not being angry with God.

The doctors could not explain it, possibly an allergic reaction to something or some type of poison. , Whatever it was, it made Joe break out with a horrible rash, turning into sores and causing constant pain. He was to sick to rebuild his business and to depressed to care. Lisa became so frustrated with their situation and blamed Joe for it telling him he had better get things straighten out with God or she was going to live with her sister. Joe was left alone, hurting, depressed, sick and tired, and he could not take anymore. Along comes his Pastor with deacons in tow!

" You know Joe, maybe you should consider asking God to forgive you, just in case you have offended him," the Pastor started off. "I ask God to forgive me everyday and I have examined myself and found nothing worthy of this," Joe explained. "Joe, I feel this may be a time to be humble before God and not self righteous," accused Deacon Brown. "You sit there and judge me, and yet you have not been here, you can not point out any way I have failed God. What right have you to accuse me?" Joe countered. Deacon Jones stepped in, "Let us use some logic here Joe. We know God is a loving God, he is just and shows mercy. But, we also know he punishes sin, and you have had so much to happen that, well, it is starting to look like you are being punished for something. Would you not agree with that?" "It is not about what you can or can not see, it is about the condition of your heart, and my heart is right with God" Joe replied.

Joe's friends, realizing they were not getting anywhere with him, left shaking their heads, and now Joe was more alone than ever and he gave in to the frustration and cried. Looking up he shouted, "God I know why people do not believe in you! How could you have let this happen to me? I understand why people do not want to become Christians, why they will not trust in you! I know that your word said you would not leave nor forsake me, but I feel alone and forsaken. I am at the end of my rope and you are not there. Why have you forsaken me? I am a good person? I do nothing wrong! I don't deserve this!" He then laid curled on the floor and cried himself to sleep.

The tree was standing in the middle of a large grass covered field. Joe sat in a swing hanging from one of the massive limbs, it was quiet and peaceful. A man in a bright white robe stood next to the tree. Joe realized the man was an angel or maybe even God himself appearing as a man, or was this a vision. Joe was the first to speak, "where have you been," he asked. The man answered, "I have been here all along Joe, right by your side." "I have not seen you there and have not felt you in a long time," Joe replied. God's voice was so soft and calm that it was easy to understand why the wind and the waves calm at the sound of it. "Joe, you have been looking at all the things happening around you and to you to see or feel me, but I have always been there." There was no pain, confusion or frustration in this field, just peace. "Father why did all this happen to me?" Joe asked. "It was a test of your faith Joe. Believing when you do not see or feel is faith. Salvation comes by faith. All that a person receives from me comes by faith. Believing in spite of circumstances and trials is faith. Believing when no one believes in you is faith. Joe, I believed in you, and you have passed the test. Your day of deliverance has come. Your restoration is here. Your healing has started". The white robed man started to glow, the warmth engulfed Joe and he woke up feeling peaceful.

It was amazing how quickly God put Joe's life back together. His stores were re-opened, Lisa moved home and they raised their grandchildren that were spared at Joe Junior's that fateful night. God healed the hurt, filled the voids, and picked them up again.

How long does it take to stop hurting? I do not know. Some have told me it takes years. One man told me he has been married for ten years and still is not over his first wife. But I do know God has been with me. He has given me little gifts along the way and is helping me heal. God can do that, we just have to give Him the pieces. Remember never give up and don't shoot the horse.

Chapter 18

Regaining Your Smile

O my soul, why be so gloomy and discouraged? Trust in God! I shall again praise him for his wondrous help; he will make me smile again, for he is my God! Psalms 43:5 (Living Bible)

Someone once said that people smile at people who smile. I found that to be true the day before we were to take Christmas leave from work. I have eight men who work for me and a supervisor who I work for. I bought my men a Christmas coffee cup and put a bag of hot chocolate and a large chocolate chip cookie in it. It was not much, but I just wanted to get them something. I was like a kid at Christmas, I went and told all of them to stop by my desk on their way to break. I stood there smiling because as they came one by one, they were surprised that I had gotten them something and it brought smiles to all there faces. My supervisor came walking up and said "Randy, what are you smiling about?" as he smiled. My crew's smile made me smile, my smile made my supervisor smile, and when the boss is happy, everybody is happy. What is so special about a smile? Let us take a look.

Believe it or not, there have been studies on smiling. The fact that researchers thought smiling was worth studying makes it worth considering for us. Smiling has benefits, not only for you but also for the people around you. Smiling brings oxygen to the brain, and makes you feel better. When you feel better you send out positive messages to others. Smiling will make you appear to be a likable person, someone pleasant to be around. When you meet people and are not smiling, they will feel you are not interested in them, or that you are a cold person. If you are not in the mood to be smiling, a fake smile may not help until someone sees you smiling, then they will smile back at you and that will make your smile authentic, so smile.

Here is some good news for those who want to look younger, smile; it will lift your face. That is a good reason to be smiling. There have been some cases that smiling lowered blood pressure and it helps you relax. Smiling can even boost your immune system. Have you noticed that happy people are not as sick as pessimistic people? Smiling naturally draws people to you. It will help you get along with others and improve relations with your employers. Did you know that a boss would most likely promote those who smile? Wouldn't you? The simple act of smiling can improve your day. So smile.

A smile costs nothing but gives much. It enriches those who receive without making poorer those who give. It takes but a moment, but the memory of it sometimes lasts forever. None is so rich or mighty that he cannot get along without it and none is so poor that he cannot be made rich by it. Yet a smile cannot be bought, begged, borrowed, or stolen, for it is something that is of no value to anyone until it is given away. Some people are too tired give you a smile. Give them yours, as none needs a smile so much he who has no more to give. (Author Unknown)

The story of Jacob and Esau is a good one and the Living Bible tells it in a wonderful way. I will leave the numbers out to make it more story like.

One day, in Isaac's old age when he was almost blind, he called for Esau his oldest son. Isaac: ``My son?'' Esau: ``Yes, father?'' Isaac: ``I am an old man now, and expect every day to be my last. Take your bow and arrows out into the fields and get me some venison, and prepare it just the way I like it--savory and good--and bring it here for me to eat, and I will give you the blessings that belong to you, my first-born son, before I die.''

But Rebekah overheard the conversation. So when Esau left for the field to hunt for the venison, she called her son Jacob and told him what his father had said to his brother.

Rebekah: ``Now do exactly as I tell you. Go out to the flocks and bring me two young goats, and I'll prepare your father's favorite dish from them. Then take it to your father, and after he has enjoyed it he will bless you before his death, instead of Esau!''

Jacob: ``But mother! He won't be fooled that easily. Think how hairy Esau is, and how smooth my skin is! What if my father feels me? He'll think I'm making a fool of him, and curse me instead of blessing me!''

Rebekah: ``Let his curses be on me, dear son. Just do what I tell you. Go out and get the goats.''

So Jacob followed his mother's instructions, bringing the dressed kids, which she prepared in his father's favorite way.

Then she took Esau's best clothes--they were there in the house--and instructed Jacob to put them on.

And she made him a pair of gloves from the hairy skin of the young goats, and fastened a strip of the hide around his neck;

then she gave him the meat, with its rich aroma, and some fresh-baked bread.

Jacob carried the platter of food into the room where his father was lying. Jacob: ``Father?'' Isaac: ``Yes? Who is it, my son--Esau or Jacob?''

Jacob: ``It's Esau, your oldest son. I've done as you told me to. Here is the delicious venison you wanted. Sit up and eat it, so that you will bless me with all your heart!''

Isaac: ``How were you able to find it so quickly, my son?''
Jacob: ``Because Jehovah your God put it in my path!''

Isaac: ``Come over here. I want to feel you, and be sure it really is Esau!''

(Jacob goes over to his father. He feels him!) Isaac: (to himself) ``The voice is Jacob's, but the hands are Esau's!''

(The ruse convinces Isaac and he gives Jacob his blessings):

Isaac: ``Are you really Esau?'' Jacob: ``Yes, of course.''

Isaac: ``Then bring me the venison, and I will eat it and bless you with all my heart.'' (Jacob takes it over to him and Isaac eats; he also drinks the wine Jacob brings him.)

Isaac: ``Come here and kiss me, my son!'' (Jacob goes over and kisses him on the cheek. Isaac sniffs his clothes, and finally seems convinced.)

Isaac: ``The smell of my son is the good smell of the earth and fields that Jehovah has blessed. May God always give you plenty of rain for your crops, and good harvests and grapes. May many nations be your slaves. Be the master of your brothers. May all your relatives bow low before you. Cursed are all who curse you, and blessed are all who bless you.''

(As soon as Isaac has blessed Jacob, and almost before Jacob leaves the room, Esau arrives, coming in from his hunting.

He also has prepared his father's favorite dish and brings it to him.) Esau: ``Here I am, father, with the venison. Sit up and eat it so that you can give me your finest blessings!''

Isaac: ``Who is it?'' Esau: ``Why, it's me, of course! Esau, your oldest son!''

(Isaac begins to tremble noticeably.) Isaac: ``Then who is it who was just here with venison, and I have already eaten it and blessed him with irrevocable blessing?''

(Esau begins to sob with deep and bitter sobs.) Esau: ``O my father, bless me, bless me too!''

Isaac: ``Your brother was here and tricked me and has carried away your blessing.''

Esau: (bitterly) ``No wonder they call him `The Cheater.' For he took my birthright, and now he has stolen my blessing. Oh, haven't you saved even one blessing for me?''

Isaac: ``I have made him your master, and have given him yourself and all of his relatives as his servants. I have guaranteed him abundance of grain and wine--what is there left to give?''

Esau: ``Not one blessing left for me? O my father, bless me too.'' (Isaac says nothing as Esau weeps.)

Isaac: ``Yours will be no life of ease and luxury, but you shall hew your way with your sword. For a time you will serve your brother, but you will finally shake loose from him and be free.''

So Esau hated Jacob because of what he had done to him. He said to himself, ``My father will soon be gone, and then I will kill Jacob.''

But someone got wind of what he was planning, and reported it to Rebekah. She sent for Jacob and told him that his life was being threatened by Esau.

``This is what to do,'' she said. ``Flee to your Uncle Laban in Haran.

Stay there with him awhile until your brother's fury is spent, and he forgets what you have done. Then I will send for you. For why should I be bereaved of both of you in one day?"

Then Rebekah said to Isaac, ``I'm sick and tired of these local girls. I'd rather die than see Jacob marry one of them." (Genesis 27)

When Jacob stole the birthright and blessing, what did he get? First he received the superior rank in his family, he also got a double portion of the paternal inheritance. he would hold the priestly office in the family, and the promise of the Seed in which all nations of the earth would be blessed.

While Jacob was staying with his uncle, he was blessed in a great way and grew rich and had a large family, but the time came when he wanted to go home. Jacob did not know how he would be received by his brother and was afraid that Esau would kill him when he got there. Here we will pick up the story in chapter forty three.

Then, far in the distance, Jacob saw Esau coming with his 400 men.

Jacob now arranged his family into a column, with his two concubines and their children at the head, Leah and her children next, and Rachel and Joseph last.

Then Jacob went on ahead. As he approached his brother he bowed low seven times before him.

And then Esau ran to meet him and embraced him affectionately and kissed him; and both of them were in tears!

Then Esau looked at the women and children and asked, ``Who are these people with you?'' ``My children,'' Jacob replied.

Then the concubines came forward with their children, and bowed low before him.

Next came Leah with her children, and bowed, and finally Rachel and Joseph came and made their bows.

``And what were all the flocks and herds I met as I came?'' Esau asked. And Jacob replied, ``They are my gifts, to curry your favor!''

``Brother, I have plenty,'' Esau laughed. ``Keep what you have.''

``No, but please accept them,'' Jacob said, ``for what a relief it is to see your friendly smile! I was as frightened of you as though approaching God!

Jacob had a right to feel shame, guilt, and fear, where his brother was concerned, after all Jacob was guilty. When Jacob grew near Esau, his fear grew until he saw Esau's face. The guilt, fear, and shame melted away under a smile. The smile of Esau told Jacob he once again had a brother, and that there was forgiveness and restoration. The smile of Esau told Jacob he had regained the family that he lost by his own actions.

A lot can be seen in a smile. A lot happens inside the person receiving a smile, and a lot happens inside the person giving a smile. So smile.

William Shakespeare said in *Othello,* "The robbed that smiles, steals something from the thief."

An Unknown Author said, "The shortest distance between two people is a smile."

Mother Teresa said, "Every time you smile at someone, it is an action of love, a gift to that person, a beautiful thing." So smile.

Chapter 19

Under the influence

A few years ago, I wrote a short story to illustrate how changing your environment will change you. Here is that story.

Little Boy Lost

There was a little boy named Russ, who loved to play in the woods. The woods were friendly; the animals were tame and comfortable with people living on the edge of the forest. Russ had friends in the woods, a little fox that would come and play with him and run along with him, as he would go on his explorations of the mighty woods. There were squirrels, raccoons, chipmunks, deer, and all kinds of birds that would come up to him and he would feed them, Russ loved to put peanuts on his shoulder and let squirrels run up his leg and back to claim the nut. All of the animals were his friends but the little fox was a companion, his best friend, the two of them were inseparable. Russ named the little fox, Foxy. Russ knew everything about the forest, the difference between a white oak and a red oak, which trees grew nuts that could

Don't Shoot the Horse

be eaten and which ones that were not very good. He even knew what plants were good for burns and how to use them. " I am a woodsman", he would proclaim. Russ would wear his coonskin hat and pretended to be a descendent of Daniel Boone. Russ would never stray to deep into the woods, but would stay close to his back yard where he knew he would be safe.

One day the woods changed, some wolves wondered into Russ' peaceful domain. Russ had no knowledge of the danger that had creped into the woods, and while exploring the forest found himself cut off from his backyard by the howling wolves. Russ ran, he ran hard and fast, without looking back or stopping to rest he ran until he could no longer hear the barking of the predators. When he finally stopped, he realized that he was lost. Russ looked around and did not recognize any familiar sights, and did not know which way to go to get home. Russ wondered around trying to find something that would point him toward home until it started to storm, the lightning and thunder frighten him, the rain poured down like standing under a waterfall. Russ ran for the nearest shelter he could find, a cave. The cave was a safe place to hide from the storm, and the wolves. When his eyes adjusted to the dim light Russ went a little deeper into the cave and discovered three little lion cubs, they were very playful and Russ started to enjoy the cave. "I only thought I was a woodsman, but I'm really a caveman," Russ would proclaim. He took his coonskin cap off and proceeded to play with the lion cubs, not even thinking that the cubs would have a mother. Mountain lions were rare in this part of the country but a few still existed and Russ had found some, and did not know the danger they posed.

When the storm subsided, it had become very late and Russ fell asleep, when he woke up, he was hungry. Somewhere in the distance, he heard the roar of the mountain lion, and was overcome with fear and ran outside the cave again looking for safety.

"Russ" someone was calling for him. "Russ" the familiar voice came again. The sound of that voice brought warmth to Russ' heart; it was the voice of his father. Russ ran toward the voice. Russ had never run so hard in his life, he ran harder for the voice than the did to flee the storm. The voice meant home, love and safety. When he got close to the sound of the voice, he started to recognize his surroundings, his beloved woods. He was home, and he was really a woodsman.

It is no secret that we will become what we hang around. That is the reason the only people who want to hear you complain are people who have something to complain about. On a more positive side, people smile at people who smile. If something as simple as a smile can influence another person's attitude then we all should be smiling.

One of my favorite Psalms is chapter 42; I want to show you a few things in this beautiful poem.

Psalms 42

1. As the hart panteth after the water brooks, so panteth my soul after thee, O God.

2. My soul thirsteth for God, for the living God: when shall I come and appear before God?

3. My tears have been my meat day and night, while they continually say unto me, Where is thy God?

4. When I remember these things, I pour out my soul in me: for I had gone with the multitude, I went with them to the house of God, with the voice of joy and praise, with a multitude that kept holyday.

The hart is a deer that will drink from the brooks and rivers, but when being hunted or chased by a predator will seek out water that is deep enough for it to completely submerse itself in and occasionally stick it's nose out for air. When you think of the Spirit of God as a mighty river and know that when we are being hunted or chased by the enemy of our souls there is a place we can submerse ourselves into where the enemy cannot reach us. The enemy is after David here and he longs for the relationship he once new with God. Where the spirit was waters to swim in.

3. My tears have been my meat day and night, while they continually say unto me, Where is thy God?

David's sorrow was so deep he could not eat; all he had was his tears. Why? Because he could no longer feel the presence of God. We know God will never leave nor forsake us; we know he is always with us even to the end of the age, but sometimes we let things come between God and us. When I was a young person in the church youth group, another youth member, Cathy, had a spiritual crisis. Cathy was dedicated to God but went through what some people call "a dry spell." She could not feel the presence of God. Young people sometimes do not understand that our salvation is simply through faith and not by what we feel. Every summer the young people would go to youth camp. While on the bus, we would sing. While singing a song with the words "God's not dead, no, He is alive," Cathy sat at the back of the bus not participating with the rest of the group singing. I asked her what was wrong and she told me she did not know if God was alive. When we got to camp, she spent the entire week in the same state of mind, until the last night when there was a special altar call, and all the young people gathered around her and pleaded with her to the alter for prayer. They asked me to speak with Cathy and when I approached her, she told me she did not know what to do. I told her that she was once close to God and she knew how to get there again. Cathy went down to the altar and experienced a Divine encounter. We prayed with her, then the rest of us went to the snack bar, we returned to the chapel to find she was still there drinking from the spring of living water. David's experience at this time is similar to Cathy's. He could not feel God, and spent day and night in mourning over his condition. David had friends like Job who came to him and said where is your God? We heard of your battle with the bear and lion and God was with you then, but where is He now?

We saw you kill the giant and God was with you then, but where is He now?

We saw you dance before the ark; God was with you then, but where is He now?

We saw you lead a kingdom with the guidance of God, Where is He now?

David was alone, and could not find God.

> *4. When I remember these things, I pour out my soul in me: for I had gone with the multitude, I went with them to the house of God, with the voice of joy and praise, with a multitude that kept holyday*

David remembered a time when he lead a group to the House of God and worshipped in the presence of God. He had been there once before and knew how to get there again. He had to find the multitude that kept holyday. The influence of the multitude kept David close to God.

One night a woman heard a noise downstairs in her house. She took a weapon and went down to see what caused the noise. When she went into the living room, she discovered a man asleep on the couch. She called the police and they arrived and went into the house without waking the man up. The police discovered that the man was drunk and had once lived in that house, and thought that he was home. It was ruled that he was *under the influence*. There are all kinds of things that influence us in life, some for the good and others for bad. Then there are times that we are an influence in the lives of others, sometimes good and other times bad.

If our lives were a book, would reading it inspire or discourage the reader? We read stories all the time about how someone was influenced by the life of someone else. Who or what influenced you is one question that is asked to most successful people, and most of the time they have an answer.

J.R.R. Tolkin was a devout Roman Catholic and had a friend named Cleve, who was an atheist. Tolkin was in the same writers group as Cleve, and they would meet and share what they were working on. Through Tolkins influence, Cleve started to consider Christianity, and eventually became a Christian. Cleve did not like his name and took the nickname of Jack, but when he wrote, he used his initials, C.S. Lewis. The creator of the Chronicles of Nadia and many other great works in Christian literature that has in turn influenced the lives of many Christians.

What would happen if we all could influence just one person that might turn out to be another C.S. Lewis? You never know when you talk to someone how far the ripples of your action will reach.

Some of the greatest Bible heroes were influence by someone who did not stand out like the people that they influenced. Andrew brought Peter to the Lord.

John 1: 40. One of the two, which heard John speak, and followed him, was Andrew, Simon Peter's brother.

41. He first fended his own brother Simon, and smith unto him, we have found the Messiahs, which is, being interpreted, the Christ.

42. And he brought him to Jesus. And when Jesus beheld him, he said, Thou art Simon the son of Jona: thou shalt be called Cephas, which is by interpretation, A stone.

When Saul/Paul became a Christian, the other Disciples were afraid of him, but a man named Barnabas went to Paul.

Acts 9:27. But Barnabas took him,(Paul) and brought him to the apostles, and declared unto them how he had seen the Lord in the way, and that he had spoken to him, and how he had preached boldly at Damascus in the name of Jesus.

28. And he was with them coming in and going out at Jerusalem.

The woman at the well brought the people of Samaria to Jesus and after the death and resurrection of Jesus, Phillip ran a revival in the city and the Bible records that there was great joy in the city. If you look closely at some of the stories in the Gospels you find them mentioned, nameless people who did their part in the Gospel. They may not be mentioned by name but God knows their names and has an award waiting for them.

People let alcohol and drugs influence them. Some let friends and peers influence them, while others let society influence them, and some even let television influence them. There are other things that influence us like love, the Bible, and even the Holy Spirit.

Have you ever let love influence you to do something? I know a man who worked with his wife and they would get home late at night. Some nights were cold and their house was not heated very well, there was no central heating just gas wall heaters and a fireplace. When they would get home on those late and cold nights he would let her nap in the car while he went in and turned on the heaters and start a fire in the fireplace, he would go into the bedroom and turn on the electric blanket so the bed would be warm, and then he would go out to the car and wake his wife up to go into a warm house. The man loved his wife and was under the influence of love. Many parents sacrifice for their children, wives for their husbands and husbands for their wives, because they are under the influence of love. It was the influence of love that held Jesus to the cross. Nails could not do it. There was no Roman solider or demonic power strong enough to drive a nail through the hand of Jesus. We are talking about the one who could control the wind and the waves with His words; we are talking about the one the demons feared upon the sight of Him. We are talking about the one who could walk on water or turn it into wine, and feed five thousand with a happy meal. The one who could make a withered hand whole, could free His hand from a nail. When I was little, there was a popular song that had words like this, "He could have called ten thousand angels to destroy the world and set him free" and He could have but did not have to. He could have done it all on his own. John tells us *He created everything there is--nothing exists that he did not make. (John 1:3 Living Bible)* He made it and can destroy it and will at the end of time. On the day of the cross, Jesus was under the influence of love, and because of that love, we could know love.

While Jesus ministered on this world, He was under the influence of the Holy Spirit.

> *Luke 4:1. And Jesus being full of the Holy Ghost returned from Jordan, and was led by the Spirit into the wilderness,*
>
> *Luke 4:18. The Spirit of the Lord is upon me, because he hath anointed me to preach the gospel to the poor; he hath sent me to heal the brokenhearted, to preach deliverance to the captives, and recovering of sight to the blind, to set at liberty them that are bruised,*

Being under the influence of the Holy Spirit is the best of all influences. It is the one that teaches us to be Christ like, encourages us to keep going when it looks like all is lost, inspires us to be compassionate to others, and strengthens us when we are weak.

I was at a friend's house for a cookout many years ago. I was walking around outside when I saw a bicycle and I climbed on the bike and road to a friends' house not far away. When

I knocked on the door, I discovered my friend was going through a depression, after spending some time there my friend said, "Wow! There is so much energy in this room you can see it." I did not know what they were talking about, but I knew there was not any depression in that house anymore. The Spirit put it in my heart that day to visit a friend and the Spirit rescued them from the pit of depression.

There was another time when I went to a friend's house to pick him up for church because his wife was working that morning and they had only one car. When I walked into the house, he was sitting on the couch and was not dressed for church. He looked up and told me his wife had asked him for a separation. I referred them to a professor for counseling. Meeting with him did not bring a solution, and they asked me for help. I followed the counseling steps and techniques I had learned in college but did not feel that I was making any headway. They were sitting on the couch and I was in a chair and the coffee table was in the middle and on the coffee table was a Bible. I was impressed to have them read Psalms 42 together. As they sat and read, tears started to feel their eyes and God preformed a divine act that day in their lives. They went on to have children and entered into the ministry. If you let the Spirit lead you, the lives of the people around you will be changed, and yours will be transformed.

If we live in the Spirit, let us also walk in the Spirit. Galatians 5:25

In Acts 16, we learn that twice Paul wanted to go one place but the Holy Spirit would not let them and through a dream led them somewhere else. We find a similar story in Acts 10 when God spoke to Peter and a man by the name of Cornelius. Cornelius needed to hear the good news and was sent to meet Peter. Peter had to learn the Gospel was for everyone and not just the Jews. The Spirit led them to each other and the Gospel was sent to Caesarea. Learning to listen to and feel the impressions of the Holy Spirit can lead us to a fulfilled life for ourselves and impact the lives of others.

How do you learn to be led by the Spirit? The answer is simple; the task is a little harder. It is easy to say that we should practice listening to the Holy Spirit, but it is sometime a little difficult to do and a little scary to step out and do something or say something on what feels like a hunch. How do you distinguish between a hunch and the impression of the Holy Spirit? First learn God's word. There you will find what God will and will not do. Second, spend time alone with God. Find a place where you are not bombarded with all the things that attack your senses and can clear your mind. When you pray spend some time in silence, meditate on God's word and you will start to have thoughts, if those thoughts match up with the Bible and the character of God and God's plan for man, you may find the Spirit is leading you.

Chapter 20

Regaining your footing

The police officer was only doing his job, and doing it right. He did not expect things would go terribly wrong as he was putting on his bulletproof vest and preparing to go out on patrol. There was a robbery that night and someone was shot at a small gas station, putting the police force on high alert. Later that night the automobile the suspect was driving was spotted and soon the police were involved in a hot pursuit. The police put spikes across the road in he path of the suspect's vehicle, in an effort to bring the chase to a safe ending. The suspect ran over the spikes and his tires blew out, causing him to lose control of the vehicle and leave the roadway. Officer Kim Carman was approaching from the opposite direction and pulled in front of the car. When the car came to a stop the suspect started firing his gun, striking Officer Kim several times in the body in areas not covered by his body armor. One entered his shoulder just above the vest and one entered his abdomen just below the vest. A third bullet went through his arm. The fourth bullet struck him center mass, but was stopped by his body armor. Officer Kim was rushed to the hospital where the bullets were removed, and he started on the road to recovery. The suspect did not survive that night; he was not wearing body armor. The point of the story is that even though Officer Kim was wearing a vest he was wounded. At first he thought that the vest had done him no good because somehow the bullets had found their way around his protection, then he learned that the bullet that had struck him in the chest would have killed him but was stopped by his body armor. When someone is hit in the chest while wearing a bulletproof vest, even though the bullet does not penetrate the armor, the impact of the bullet is like a blow from a sledge hammer, it will knock them off of their feet and sometime make them lose consciousness.

Sometimes we are hit so hard by the circumstances of life it knocks us down and sometimes knocks the breath out of us, even when we are wearing the armor of God. Let us take a look at the armor and see if there is anything, we can do to help our armor from being pierced.

> *Ephesians 6: 11. Put on the whole armour of God, that ye may be able to stand against the wiles of the devil.*
>
> *12. For we wrestle not against flesh and blood, but against principalities, against powers, against the rulers of the darkness of this world, against spiritual wickedness in high places.*
>
> *13. Wherefore take unto you the whole armour of God, that ye may be able to withstand in the evil day, and having done all, to stand.*
>
> *14. Stand therefore, having your loins girt about with truth, and having on the breastplate of righteousness;*

15. And your feet shod with the preparation of the gospel of peace;

16. Above all, taking the shield of faith, wherewith ye shall be able to quench all the fiery darts of the wicked.

17. And take the helmet of salvation, and the sword of the Spirit, which is the word of God:

When Paul wrote the book of Ephesians, he was under house arrest in Rome and was escorted constantly by a Roman soldier, so he was very familiar with the armor of the Roman soldier. When he said put on the whole armor of God he meant to take advantage of all of God's protective resources. Wearing just the helmet of salvation would not suffice living in a world falling under the influence of the enemy. The devil often attacks the heart or other vital parts of our being. We have to make sure that there are no gaps in our armor. David found a flaw in the armor of Goliath. Satan can certainly find flaws in our armor. We have to work to make our armor as flawless as possible. What did Paul mean when he said that we should wear the armor so we would be able to stand against the wiles of the devil? The word wiles means trickery, the Greek word is methodeia and denotes a path that is traveled over, or a method. The method of the devil is trickery and he is constantly traveling that road to interfere with our relationship with God.

Paul tells us that our fight is not with flesh and blood but against spiritual wickedness. James tells us that if we resist the devil that he will flee from us. We can defeat the devil by resistance. The devil uses trickery to pull the rug out from under us. By putting on the whole armor of God we can regain our footing to take a stand of resistance against the devil's methods of attack.

Stand therefore, having your loins girt about with truth, Ephesians 6:14.

The belt of truth is possibly the most important piece of armor. You may be thinking that a belt would not be very valuable in a battle, but the belt is where you hang your sword, prop your shield, and secures your breastplate. The belt may not hold your helmet on and may not attach to the shoes, but a soldier would look pretty ridiculous going to battle wearing nothing but his hat and shoes. Truth, on the other hand, is very important to salvation and the Gospel. What does the Bible say about truth? A lot, look and see.

John 1:14. And the Word was made flesh, and dwelt among us, (and we beheld his glory, the glory as of the only begotten of the Father,) full of grace and **truth.**

John 1:17. For the law was given by Moses, but grace and **truth** *came by Jesus Christ.*

John 8: 32. And ye shall know the **truth***, and the* **truth** *shall make you free.*

John 14:6. Jesus saith unto him, I am the way, the **truth***, and the life: no man cometh unto the Father, but by me.*

John 17:17. Sanctify them through thy **truth***: thy word is* **truth.**

All of these verses are from the book of John, there are a lot more in the Bible, but most are in the book of John.

The foundation for salvation is that the Gospels are truth, that Jesus was born of a virgin, lived a sinless life and died on a cross for our sins. If you do not believe in the truth of the Gospels then the armor would be useless to you, there would be nothing to hold it all together. Without the truth of the Gospel, we would be helpless to the attacks of the devil.

Pilate ask Jesus the question "what is truth", I understand why he asked that question. Pilate could find no fault in Jesus and yet he was going to be crucified, Pilate was willing to let Jesus go, but his own people did not want it. Jesus was faultless but the people chose to let a robber go free. When Jesus said everyone that is of the truth hears my voice, and everyone was turning from him, Pilate saw no truth. It was not long after that, Jesus rose from the dead and the truth spread like wildfire throughout the world. The truth is still there, it is all wrapped up in the person of Jesus Christ. When we accept Jesus and all that he said and did, and follow his example, we are wearing the belt of truth.

Ephesians 6:14. Stand therefore, and having on the breastplate of righteousness;

The breastplate protected the heart, and other vital organs. Have you ever wished that there was something to protect your heart? I would dare to say that there have been as many people to lose faith from a broken heart as anything else that the devil throws at us. When a person is hurt in church, or by a person, or disappointed by a pastor or teacher or maybe even a friend or spouse it breaks their heart. Satan uses our fragile heart to make us lose faith in God, which is why the heart needs to be protected. How do we protect the heart?

It is easy to say put on the breastplate of righteousness, but how do you do it. What is righteousness? Righteousness is being made right, or being in the right standing before God. It is the same as justification, or being made just with God, or being found innocent. The first way we become righteous is simple, accept Jesus as your personal Lord and Savior.

> *Genesis 15:6. And he believed in the Lord; and he counted it to him for righteousness.*

As early as Abraham in Genesis, believing in God brought righteousness. Righteousness is a gift from God that we receive when we believe.

> *Genesis 5:17. If, because of one man's trespass, death reigned through that one man, much more will those who receive the abundance of grace and the free gift of righteousness reign in life through the one man Jesus Christ. (RSV)*

We are given the breastplate of righteousness when we become Christians; how we wear that breastplate is up to us. Wear it loosely and we make room for the fiery darts of the devil to get through. Just receiving the breastplate of righteousness is not enough. In biblical times, the breastplate was made to fit the Roman soldier, but we must conform to the breastplate. What I mean by this is we must also live righteous lives. We were made righteous by faith in Jesus Christ; our lives need to show our righteousness to the world. Our righteous living strengthens the breastplate and makes us stronger. Some of the synonyms for righteousness are virtuous, moral, good, upright, honest, honorable, and respectable. The more righteous a person lives, the less ammunition the devil has to war against them. Someone once said that honesty requires no memory, so living in truth and righteousness makes for a more worry free life. So live right!

And your feet shod with the preparation of the gospel of peace. Two men went hiking, one wore his rugged hiking boots and the other showed up in a pair of running shoes. "Why in the world did you wear running shoes to go hiking?" the first man asked. "In case we come across a bear," the second man replied. "Don't you know that you can not out run a bear even in those?." Mr. Running shoes answered him by saying "I do not have to out run the bear, just you". Both men made preparations for the hiking trip; they just had different things in mind while making their preparations. What should we have in mind in making preparation of the Gospel of peace? In the Greek, the words mean exactly what they say in English, preparation means to prepare, Gospel means good news, and peace means peace, so there is no hidden meaning to reveal. Therefore, this is an opportunity to tell what I think about all this.

I heard a couple of people talking about buying a handgun. One of them commented that everyone should own a pistol, and asked my opinion. I said that I tried to stay out of places where I would need a pistol. There are some places I have heard about that if you went there they would search you, and if you did not have a gun they would give you one. I do not go to those places. I believe in peace. Paul said that if it is possible, live peaceably with all men. In other words, do not be a troublemaker, do not look for trouble and when ever possible avoid trouble. STAY OUT OF TROUBLE. I was once done terribly wrong, and had to face the wrong doer on a daily basis, I had almost every man tell me that I was a better man that they were because they would have come in like "walking tall" and cleaned house. I was able to tell them that it was because of my faith in God that I was able to refrain from such actions. My pain was obvious, the wrong done to me was evident, but it was my faith that spoke the loudest. I am not bragging, I am testifying to the power of the grace of God. I wanted to be a troublemaker, I wanted to get revenge, to get even. God wanted to be seen and He is bigger than I am.

The Gospel is "good news". The good news that Jesus came and died for us and brought salvation, healing, and peace to everyone that will simply receive it from him. Accept the Gospel and all that it offers and we will be able to stand, and when a time come that we are knocked off our feet, we will be able to stand back up and face the challenges of. Your feet, being shod with the preparation of the Gospel of peace are the foundation of your faith. Learn all you can about the gospel, build a large and deep foundation, get up and stand on it and you will be able to stand strong.

16. Above all, taking the shield of faith, wherewith ye shall be able to quench all the fiery darts of the wicked.

There are a lot of different kinds of shields; anyone who has watched television or seen pictures in books has seen small round shields, long body length shields and those that we recognize as shield shaped shields. They came with many different designs on them, during the crusades, many had the image of a cross, and others would have a family crest on them, or some emblem that had a specific meaning. The Roman soldier would carry a long shield that would cover the entire body; the shield would be made of layers of wood so that the weight would be less then one made of metal. The shield was curved so the missiles of the enemy would be parried to the side and the solider would not absorb the full force of the impact. The shield is called the shield of faith; the important thing here is in whom you put your faith.

The God of my rock; in him will I trust: He is my shield, and the Horn Of my salvation, my high tower, and my refuge, my saviour; thou savest me from violence. (2nd Samuel 22:3)

Throughout the Old Testament God is referred to as our shield. I can not think of anyone or anything I would rather stand behind than God. I can not think of anything that can protect me from the attacks of the devil as well as God. The shield of faith, what is faith? Faith is the substance of things hoped for, the evidence of things not seen. (Hebrews 11:1) Faith is believing, believing that God is with you, will protect you, and has your best interest at heart. Because I believe, I will continue to pray in the midst of hopeless situations. Because I believe, I will live for God when all around me are living for self. Because I believe, I will continue to teach the love and grace of Jesus Christ. Because I believe, I will stand for God and everything that means. I believe in God and He is my shield. Do you believe? Will you stand with me?

17. And take the helmet of salvation.

The helmet of salvation is very important. It sits on the head, protecting the mind. Romans 12:2 tells us to be transformed by the renewing of the mind. Salvation comes not only to the heart but also to the mind. Salvation should change the very way we think. Our negative attitudes should become positive, our general outlook should be one of hope and a bright future. The Roman helmet was the piece of armor that stood out the most, just as our salvation should. The helmet was plumed with brightly colored feathers or dyed horsehair. The purpose of the plume was to identify, some may have shown rank or family ties, or even the regiment that the solider was with. Our plume marks our family ties. We are a part of God's family, and our helmets should be worn with dignity and integrity. Someone who believed in astrology asked what sign I was born under. I told them that I was born under the sign of the cross because I had been born again. Our sign, or plume is our Christ like nature. Because we wear the helmet of salvation, people should be able to see Jesus in us, and it should be such a beautiful sight that they would want a helmet like yours. We can show them how to get one.

The sword of the Spirit, which is the word of God: The sword is an offensive weapon. All the other armor is to protect. If a soldier only had protective gear, the enemy would have nothing to fear from him. Our enemy should greatly fear us because we have the means to defeat him and his evil plans. Jesus defeated Satan during the wilderness temptations by quoting the scripture. He has given us more scripture to use; our sword has gotten bigger and sharper. He also has given us the Holy Spirit to bring back to remembrance the scripture that we have learned. The problem is the sword that is kept in the scabbard. True swordsmen would practice many hours every day to become masters of their weapon, their lives depended on it. Do you practice with the word, do you study it, memorize it? Jesus did not reach into his back pocket and pull out his Gideon New Testament to do battle with the devil. He had the word in His heart, and in His mind, and was able to pull it out in a flash and cut the devil to the bone.

Thy word have I hid in mine heart, that I might not sin against thee. (Psalms 119:11)

There is nothing wrong with being hit by an assault of the devil, it happens to all of us. Sometimes we are hit so hard it knocks us down. We should never stay down but get back up and polish our armor, sharpen our swords and make a stand. When we have done all we can to keep standing, we should not lose hope. It is at those times that God will hold us up. Never give up the fight. Remember you are not in this alone, you have brothers and sister in God that will help when you are tired that will guard when you need a breather, just do not stop, you will be needed to stand guard when someone else grows weary of the battle, do not let them down, you will need them someday.

Chapter 21

The Bethesda Syndrome

§

1. After this there was a feast of the Jews; and Jesus went up to Jerusalem.

2. Now there is at Jerusalem by the sheep market a pool, which is called in the Hebrew tongue Bethesda, having five porches.

3. In these lay a great multitude of impotent folk, of blind, halt, withered, waiting for the moving of the water.

4. For an angel went down at a certain season into the pool, and troubled the water: whosoever then first after the troubling of the water stepped in was made whole of whatsoever disease he had.

5. And a certain man was there, which had an infirmity thirty and eight years.

6. When Jesus saw him lie, and knew that he had been now a long time in that case, he saith unto him, Wilt thou be made whole?

7. The impotent man answered him, Sir, I have no man, when the water is troubled, to put me into the pool: but while I am coming, another steppeth down before me.

8. Jesus saith unto him, Rise, take up thy bed, and walk.

9. And immediately the man was made whole, and took up his bed, and walked: and on the same day was the sabbath. John 5:1-9

I love the story of the man at the pool of Bethesda, and if we take a closer look at it, we may see our society, our churches and possibly sometimes ourselves.

Let us clear up the controversy of this story first. There are those that believe there was not an angel stirring the water, that it was just a legend of that time, and that God does not work on a first come first serve basis. I just happen to be one of those people that believe the Bible. If the Bible tells us an angel stirred the water, then in my thinking an angel stirred the water. I like it simple, don't you?

Why would God allow an angel to stir the water, and the first person in the pool would be healed?

Maybe because one day, the Savior Isaiah talked about who would bear our healing by His strips, would come upon the scene and change everything. Healing would be found at the foot of the cross and not in a pool. That a savior would come to deliver them from all their diseases, set them free from all their bondages, and heal their sin sick souls.

Could this pool have been a taste of things to come, a picture of the river of water that would be in us? I think the pool pointed to Jesus, the Savior that would make a way for all and not just the quick.

Let us start with verse five. We will go back and look at some of the other versus later.

And a certain man was there, which had an infirmity thirty and eight years.

This man had been sick for a long time. He was at the pool but he was not trying to get in. What was the problem? He had accepted his state, "this is the way it is and this is the way it will always be," or "what's the use, nothing will ever change." Sometimes people do not work through circumstances because they grow accustom to it, or they do not feel they can handle a change. Some people would not receive the attention they get if their affirmatives were not a part of them. It is sad to say, but some people feed off of statements such as "poor thing" and as long as they are getting your sympathy, they feel like you care and love them. That may be the reason Jesus said to him in verse six *Wilt thou be made whole.* Do you even want to be whole? Some people would rather be able to park in the handicap spaces than be able to walk. The attention people get when they are down is so valuable to them that they do not want to be up. It seems that some are more proud of their disabilities than they are their abilities. Paul said in Philippians 4:13 *I can do all things through Christ which strengtheneth me.* It is this attitude that gives us an artist that paints with his teeth, one armed baseball pitchers, one legged marathon runners, blind writers and musicians, and a multitude of others that would not let their handicaps hold them back.

Where did Jesus find the man? He was at a pool *where a great multitude of impotent folk, of blind, halt, withered, waiting for the moving of the water.* He admits later he could not get into the pool, so why was he there? Maybe, because that is where people with infirmities would gather. It is true that "misery loves company." If you sit around with a group of people and start talking about your aching back, or sinus problems, before long everyone is sharing all their health problems, and everyone feels worse when the leave than when they arrived. Maybe that is why he had been sick for thirty-eight years. There was no encouragement going on at the pool, no one to say, "it's going to be OK." There was no one smiling and spreading warmth. There was no laughter, no gentle touch, and no caring until Jesus came on the scene.

Do you even want to be healed? When Jesus asked that question, the response was not "of course" but an excuse. *7. The impotent man answered him, Sir, I have no man, when the water is troubled, to put me into the pool.* It is easier to come up with an excuse than to take responsibility for your actions or inaction. "I did not have the opportunities that others had" maybe not, but you probably had some opportunities that others did not have. I heard a professional boxer say one time that he did not lose the fight he just lost the first ten rounds. Now that is an attitude. None of us are losers. God has given everyone certain talents, it may not be singing or running with a football 100 yards, but it may be cooking for the homeless, or cleaning for the elderly, or reading at the nursing home. The person lying in a hospital bed can look over at his roommate and be an encouragement and company. The person who cannot speak can pat someone on the back. It is not about what you cannot do or the opportunities you did not have but what you can do and taking advantage of the opportunities, you do have. The person who says, "I have no education so I cannot teach" needs to remember that the disciples had no formal education, they just spent a lot of time with Jesus. *but while I am coming, another steppeth down before me.* I have no one to help me, was his first excuse, my opportunities are given to someone else, was his second excuse. If you want to sing and are never given the chance to sing at church, sing at home, your family needs to hear you. If you want to teach but there are no classes available, teach your children or friends, it may be one on one but the lesson may be passed on to many. I have sat in church services and heard the preacher teach something I mentioned to him weeks before. You never know where your little lessons will end up or how many people will hear it and pass it on. Do not begrudge the person who seems to get all the chances in life, be grateful for the ones you get. I used to have a one minute Bible story that people could call and listen to on the telephone, it was called "dial a story", there was one little boy who would call everyday, when asked what he wanted to be when he grew up he said "he wanted to be a minister like Brother Randy." I do not know where he is today or what kind of life he is living, but one day God will remind him of a dream he once had, if He has not already, and a little boy who used to listen to stories over the telephone will change lives. If you look close in the Bible you will find a lot of people are mentioned by name, but there are a lot of "they and them," they brought to Jesus the sick, Jesus taught them, nameless people who did a lot of good and helped change the world. It is not that you are in the spotlight that matters; it is the light in you that needs to shine.

What are the symptoms of the Bethesda syndrome? Let us look again, just in case you missed them.

1. Hanging around a lot of negative influence

2. Sitting around doing nothing, waiting on a miracle from God.

3. Accepting your state (things will never change)

4. Blaming others for your condition

5. Not given opportunities

Do you have any of these symptoms? You see them everywhere. Individuals certainly have them. Our society as a whole shows them. I even see them in many of our churches.

What was Jesus' answer?

> *8. Jesus saith unto him, Rise, take up thy bed, and walk.*

If Jesus had only said "rise," the man would have been healed. Would the problem have been solved? No! It was not only his physical state but also his mental state that had to be dealt with. TAKE UP YOUR BED, get your act together, AND WALK, do something. Nothing ever gets better by doing nothing. When King Hezekiah was lying in his bed dying, what could he do? He turned to face the wall and cried out to God, and God gave him fifteen more years. He could have laid there and died but he did not, he did all he could do, and lived. There is always something that can be done. Just don't shoot the horse.

Chapter 22

The End

If you were to view a believer's life as a book, the funeral of that person would not be the end of the book but the conclusion of the first chapter. I believe there is much more to come. *II Corinthians 5:8. We are confident, I say, and willing rather to be absent from the body, and to be present with the Lord.* When we leave the body, we enter the presence of Jesus. Where is Jesus? He is not in the grave anymore, He arose. He is not in a resting place, or holding place. Stephen discovered were Jesus was just before he was stoned.

> *Acts 7:55. But he, being full of the Holy Ghost, looked up stedfastly into heaven, and saw the glory of God, and Jesus standing on the right hand of God,*
>
> *56. And said, Behold, I see the heavens opened, and the Son of man standing on the right hand of God.*
>
> *Luke 24:51. And it came to pass, while he blessed them, he was parted from them, and carried up into heaven.*

> *Hebrews 9:24. For Christ is not entered into the holy places made with hands, which are the figures of the true; but into heaven itself, now to appear in the presence of God for us:*

When Jesus comes back, He will come from heaven.

> *1 Thessalonians 5:16. For the Lord himself shall descend from heaven with a shout.*

To be absent from the body is to be present with Christ and Christ is in Heaven. That means to me, when we leave this body we go to heaven. You have heard the stories, when believers die they see angels or loved ones that have gone on before. I have a cousin that lost a child to a tragic accident and years later when she was taken by cancer as she slipped into eternity she smiled. Who do you think she saw that made her smile? I think she saw her child. What will heaven be like? Revelation gives us a small glimpse of it, described in the Living Bible.

> *Revelation 4:1. Then as I looked, I saw a door standing open in heaven, and the same voice I had heard before, that sounded like a mighty trumpet blast, spoke to me and said, ``Come up here and I will show you what must happen in the future!''*
>
> *2. And instantly I was, in spirit, there in heaven and saw--oh, the glory of it!--a throne and someone sitting on it!*
>
> *3. Great bursts of light flashed forth from him as from a glittering diamond, or from a shining ruby, and a rainbow glowing like an emerald encircled his throne.*

4. Twenty-four smaller thrones surrounded his, with twenty-four Elders sitting on them; all were clothed in white, with golden crowns upon their heads.

5. Lightning and thunder issued from the throne, and there were voices in the thunder. Directly in front of his throne were seven lighted lamps representing the seven-fold Spirit of God.

6. Spread out before it was a shiny crystal sea.

Remember the chapter on regaining your wow, if the chapter did not help you to achieve it, when you get to heaven you will really experience it. While you wait for the end of time, you will be so overcome with the glories of heaven that it will not be a wait at all. I think heaven is outside of time anyway, so you probably will not be able to take everything in. This all happens in chapter two, and then comes chapter three in the book of the believer's life.

What happens in chapter three? *Revelation19:7. Let us be glad and rejoice and honor him; for the time has come for the wedding banquet of the Lamb, and his bride has prepared herself. (Living Bible)* Who is the bride of Christ? You are, that is if you are a believer. This is the time Jesus will come back and receive the bride unto himself. While the world is going through the judgment that will be poured out on it, the bride will be experiencing the wedding banquet.

1st Corinthians 15:51. Behold, I shew you a mystery; We shall not all sleep, but we shall all be changed,

52. In a moment, in the twinkling of an eye, at the last trump: for the trumpet shall sound, and the dead shall be raised incorruptible, and we shall be changed.

53. For this corruptible must put on incorruption, and this mortal must put on immortality.

54. So when this corruptible shall have put on incorruption, and this mortal shall have put on immortality, then shall be brought to pass the saying that is written, Death is swallowed up in victory.

55. O death, where is thy sting? O grave, where is thy victory?

1ˢᵗ Thessalonians 5: 13. But I would not have you to be ignorant, brethren, concerning them which are asleep, that ye sorrow not, even as others which have no hope.

*14. For if we believe that Jesus died and rose again, even so them also which sleep in Jesus will God **bring** with him.*

15. For this we say unto you by the word of the Lord, that we which are alive and remain unto the coming of the Lord shall not prevent them which are asleep.

*16. For the Lord himself shall descend from heaven with a shout, with the voice of the archangel, and with the trump of God: **and the dead in Christ shall rise first:***

17. Then we which are alive and remain shall be caught up together with them in the clouds, to meet the Lord in the air: and so shall we ever be with the Lord.

18. Wherefore comfort one another with these words.

You saw that two things happened in these verses. First, God brings those that have died in Christ back with Him and the dead in Christ will rise first, incorruptible. Then we are changed in a moment. The person we lose in chapter one comes back in chapter three, we lose nothing. I know there is a lot of different teachings on this matter and some disagree with my thinking, but I believe in hope and that God is the God of hope. I feel to believe that God would allow us to go through the judgment that will be poured out from heaven, would leave us without hope for the end time, and God will never leave us without hope. I know this is not a great theological argument. But I also know the God who rescued me from sin will keep me from the persecution that comes from heaven, but may allow me to go through persecution that comes from the world and Satan. Chapter three in the believer's life is one of great celebration. Chapter four starts with a battle in which Satan is bound for a thousand years. What happens during this thousands years? The best description we find in the book of Isaiah.

4. But with righteousness shall he judge the poor, and reprove with equity for the meek of the earth: and he shall smite the earth: with the rod of his mouth, and with the breath of his lips shall he slay the wicked.

5. And righteousness shall be the girdle of his loins, and faithfulness the girdle of his reins.

6. The wolf also shall dwell with the lamb, and the leopard shall lie down with the kid; and the calf and the young lion and the fatling together; and a little child shall lead them.

7. And the cow and the bear shall feed; their young ones shall lie down together: and the lion shall eat straw like the ox.

8. And the sucking child shall play on the hole of the asp, and the weaned child shall put his hand on the cockatrice' den.

9. They shall not hurt nor destroy in all my holy mountain: for the earth shall be full of the knowledge of the Lord, as the waters cover the sea. (Isaiah 11:4-9)

A person may live for seventy or eighty years, some longer and others not as long, but if they die in Christ, they have another thousand years coming. That is hope. The thousand years is not the last chapter either. Chapter five starts with a short season where Satan is let loose to tempt, and then comes the end of the devil when he is cast into the lake of fire and there is a new heaven and a new earth. Then comes libraries filled with chapters on the life of a believer, chapters I cannot even imagine. Never give up. The believer wins even over death and the devil. Hang in there and never shoot the horse.

Study Guides

If you read anything in the chapters of this book that inspired you, or you feel worthy to be taught to a Sunday School class, or youth group, or any other group that you may teach, I have included outlines for all of the lessons in this book. The lessons in this book are ones that I learned the hard way and it is my prayer that by sharing them that someone will be helped in their times of crisis. Maybe someone will be able to look at some things with a sense of humor, or get a glimpse of understanding, or encouragement. I believe that there is always hope. There is always reason to hang on to your faith, and reason to believe that God is working in our behalf. I have shared my heart in these pages and if you can share with your class or church then the message will go beyond these pages. That will be a good thing.

Remember that all things work together for our good.

In Christ,

H. Randy Hayes

Chapter 1

Don't Shoot the Horse

Introduction:

Shooting a horse because it has a broken leg does not solve the problem.

Problems are not what they appear to be

As big as the appear to be

Not as impossible as they project themselves to be

David and Goliath:

First Samuel 17:4

The devil has champions

Fear- Confusion- Hopelessness- disease- Divorce- Hurt- Disappointments

Phil. 2:9 The name of Jesus above every name

First Samuel 17:5&6

Giants look invincible

Do not fret over impossibilities

All things are possible Through God

First Samuel 17: 26

Develop an attitude toward your enemy

First Samuel 17:33

Discouraging counsel

First Samuel 17:34-36

Remember past victories

Personal and Biblical

God is not a respecter of persons

First Samuel 17:40

Why five stones

Preparing for a fight

First Samuel 17:48-51

Overcoming problems

Get on top

Use the sword

Chapter 2

Yelling into the Refrigerator

Introduction:

Situation comedies based on jumping to conclusions

Many problems evolve form jumping from few facts to a wrong conclusion

Second Corinthians 10:5

Bringing into captivity every <u>thought</u> to the obedience of Christ;

Second Corinthians 2:11

Lest Satan should get an advantage of us: for we are not ignorant of his <u>devices.</u>

Greek word for thought and devices is *noema*

Thoughts are a device of Satan

Things that pop into our minds

Late night call

Hanging up

Example: If a woman answers, hang up

A number found in pants pocket

Sees husband speaking to woman

There is always at least one fact in every case that we do not know.

Judge not

Genesis 6:5-7

Imaginations helped bring about the down fall and destruction of mankind

Let God feed our dreams

Fuel our thoughts

Ignite our imaginations

Philippians 4:8

Finally, brethren, whatsoever things are true, whatsoever things are honest, whatsoever things are just, whatsoever things are pure, whatsoever things are lovely, whatsoever things are of good report; if there be any virtue, and if there be any praise, think on these things.

Ephesians 3:20

Now unto him that is able to do exceeding abundantly above all that we ask or think, according to the power that worketh in us,

Good thoughts= good conclusions

Chapter 3

When Words Fall Short

Introduction:

Just like a small child trying to ring a basketball goal, many times our words fall short.

Words:

Wise counsel

Comforting words

Enlightening words

Cannot be heard over the confusion of tragedy

Psalms 139: 7-10

7. Whither shall I go from thy spirit? Or whither shall I flee from thy presence? 8. If I ascend up into heaven, thou art there: if I make my bed in hell, behold, thou art there.

9. If I take the wings of the morning, and dwell in the uttermost parts of the sea;

10. Even there shall thy hand lead me, and thy right hand shall hold me.

Being there:

Hurting people draw strength from our presence

Galatians 6:2

Bear ye one another's burdens, and so fulfil the law of Christ.

Chapter 4

What Happen to the Fish?

Introduction:

When a little child asks you a question that you can not answer, it can be a humbling experience.

Humility:

A freedom from arrogance that grows out of the recognition that all we have and are comes from God. (Nelson's New Bible Dictionary)

> *It does not matter how big you are or how great your accomplishments are, there is always someone that has soared to greater heights.*

Greatest example:

Jesus

John 1:2-3

Philippians 2: 6-8

The Greatest:

Born in a stable

Laid in a manger

Became a baby

Gave up life

Proverbs 22:4. By humility and the fear of the Lord are riches, and honour, and life.

Humility- a key to blessing

Proverbs 15: 33. The fear of the Lord is the instruction of wisdom; and before honour is humility.

Humility strengthens relationship with God

> 1st *Peter 5:5 Likewise, ye younger, submit yourselves unto the elder. Yea, all of you be subject one to another, and be clothed with humility: for God resisteth the proud, and giveth grace to the humble.*

It is by God's Grace that we become anything

Chapter 5

It Should not Happen This Way

Introduction:

Life is full of disappointments, opening the Christmas present to find pajamas is a disappointment, but we still wait for Christmas morning and the chance to open gifts.

Disappointments and surprises, mountains and valleys, day and night, cold and warmth, one makes the other worth while, one makes the other appreciated.

Bible Heroes:

Joseph expected- mighty ruler

Found slavery

Genesis Chapter 37

Joseph the favorite

Brothers the jealous

Joseph the slave

Genesis Chapters 39-42

Joseph the servant

Joseph the prisoner

Joseph the ruler

Jonah expected- righteous judgment

Found forgiveness

Prodigal son - expected great adventure

Found destitution

Joseph- disappointment in family

Jonah- disappointment in God

Prodigal- disappointment in self

Disappointment in family, God, or yourself of maybe your job, friends, or how life has turned out in general, the answer is simple, give yourself to God, He can turn things around.

Chapter 6

Christ like in Short Shorts

Introduction:

We are taught that we are not suppose to judge, but we do, we judge people by what we see. A young woman wearing shorts standing next to a woman dressed in a long dress and hair piled up on top of her head our first impression would be that the woman in the long dress would be the Christian. If we could not see them, but could only go by their attitudes we might make a different judgment.

John 7:24 Judge not according to the appearance, but judge righteous judgment.

What we wear does not show what we are:

Disciples Wear:

Not Christian slogan Tee shirts

Not Jesus ball caps

Not little fish on the donkey's hip.

Wore attitude of Christ

Isaiah 61:10. I will greatly rejoice in the Lord, my soul shall be joyful in my God; for he hath clothed me with the garments of salvation, he hath covered me with the robe of righteousness, as a bridegroom decketh himself with ornaments, and as a bride adorneth herself with her jewels.

We should wear:

Salvation

Righteousness

Humility

First Peter 5:5 Likewise, ye younger, submit yourselves unto the elder. Yea, all of you be subject one to another, and be clothed with humility: for God resisteth the proud, and giveth grace to the humble.

Chapter 7

Beyond the Shadow of a Cloud

Introduction:

Just like clouds that cover the sky from horizon to horizon, sometimes life's upsets and tragedies cover our lives and we can not see the end of them or a break in the hurting. The sun always breaks through the clouds and the face of God will always break through all the sad events of our lives.

Hosea 2:15

God turns valleys of trouble into doors of hope

He leads through valleys

God provides ways of escape

Hosea = Salvation

Gomer the temple prostitute

(Salvation marries prostitute)

People belong to God but worship other things

Jezreel = God will sow

Lo-Ruhamah = no more mercy

Lo-Ammi = not mine

Gomer becomes slave

Hosea buys her back

Hope = Confident trust that something will happen.

Not wishful thinking

A Christian has hope because God

Is the Healer

Is the Deliverer

Is the comforter

Is the Blessing Giver

Deuteronomy 28: 1-8

Hope for the Christian is Faith

All things work together for good

> *Psalms 42:5 Why art thou cast down, O my soul? and why art thou disquieted in me? hope thou in God: for I shall yet praise him for the help of his countenance.*

Chapter 8

Raped by Bitterness

Introduction: Bitterness is being resentful or angry even hostile, it is caused by pain or grief that is hard to bear.

What does it mean to a Christian?

It interferes with your relationship with God

It causes you to miss out on blessing

Hebrews 12:15

The root of bitterness

Chokes out fruit of the Spirit

Allows bitterness to grow into hate and cruelty

Seed of bitterness is unforgiveness

Matthew 6:14-15

Will God forgive unforgiveness?

Parable of the unforgiving creditor

John 15:12 John 14:24 unforgiveness shows our lack of love for Jesus

Unforgiveness hinders our physical and emotional health

Holding on to offense

Forgiveness:

Joseph

Betrayed by brothers - sold as a slave

Betrayed by Potiphar's wife - went to prison

Did not build bitterness - build a life

> *In all of his trails Joseph learned to see God at work in his life and that God was in control of his destiny.*

Forgiveness offers freedom to worship God unhindered by the past.

Learning to Forgive:

Forbearing one another, and forgiving one another, if any man have a quarrel against any: even as Christ forgave you, so also do ye. (Colossians 3:13)

To know how to forgive you need to be forgiven

1st Step - Be filled with the love of Christ

2nd Step - Choose to forgive

Ephesians 4:31-32

3rd Step - Think on good things

4th Step - Say it "I forgive you"

Saying it helps you to accept it

Chapter 9

Behind the Slow Driver

Introduction:

Have you ever wondered why the slow driver is always in front? Do you get upset with bad drivers? The problem may not be bad drivers but little patience; it is not them but you.

Patience: *willingness to put up with waiting, pain, or anything that annoys, troubles, or hurts; calm endurance without complaining or losing self-control* (*World Book Dictionary*)

> Hebrews 6:12 *That ye be not slothful, but followers of them who through faith and patience inherit the promises*

Instant in not instant

There is always a process

Instant potatoes:

Planted

Harvested

Cooked

Processed

Boxed

Shipped

First Corinthians 15:6:

500 at witnessed resurrected Savior

10 days of waiting

120 in the upper room

> *James 1:3 Knowing this, that the trying of your faith worketh patience.*

Patience in little things

Miss some of the trials

Patience could have shortened Israel's journey

Learn the lesson the first time

Noah

120 years building the ark

No converts

Seven days waiting in the ark

Forty days of rain

Floating 150 days

Luke 21:19 In your patience possess ye your souls.

Abraham, friend of God

Failed in patience

World still paying for his lack of patience

Best example- God

Paslms 86:15. But thou, O Lord, art a God full of compassion, and gracious, longsuffering, and plenteous in mercy and truth

1st Timothy 1:16. Howbeit for this cause I obtained mercy, that in me first Jesus Christ might shew forth all longsuffering, for a pattern to them which should hereafter believe on him to life everlasting.

2nd Peter 3:9. The Lord is not slack concerning his promise, as some men count slackness; but is longsuffering to us-ward, not willing that any should perish but that all should come to repentance.

God is patient toward us

Be patient or be a patient

Chapter 10

We All Have Shoes

Introduction:

If you could understand someone else's feelings by wearing their shoes,

What would happen if you tried on the shoes of Jesus?

> *Galatians 3:27. For as many of you as have been baptized into Christ have put on Christ.* Put on the compassion of Christ

Put on the understanding of Christ

Would there be a difference in you

We all have shoes:

Everyone has experience, good and bad

Do not know individuals pain but you know pain

The Savior:

Knows every kind of heart

Christ lives in us

Chapter 11

Why a Manger

Introduction:

What did Jesus get for Christmas? There were no presents that night. (The wise men came later)

Luke 2: 7 And she brought forth her firstborn son, and wrapped him in swaddling clothes, and laid him in a manger; because there was no room for them in the inn.

Hebrews 4:15. For we have not an high priest which cannot be touched with the feeling of our infirmities; but was in all points tempted like as we are, yet without sin.

Temptations of Jesus:

Confrontation with parents at age 12

Joseph goes missing

The wilderness temptation:

Matthew 4:3 The lust of the flesh

Tempted to misuse his power

Eve in the garden Genesis 3:6

Second wilderness temptation:

Matthew 4:6

The pride of life

Temptation at the house of God

Eve, you will be like God

"Look at me"

Third wilderness temptation

Matthew 4:8 and 9 Lust of the eyes

Jesus saw everything the world has to offer

Eve saw the tree was pleasant to the eyes

Luke 4:13. And when the devil had ended all the temptation, he departed from him for a season.

The devil left for a season, he most likely came back to tempt again.

Chapter 12

Stories Told to Me

There is no outline for this chapter. The Bible verse Psalms 3:11 is a powerful one. I relate these stories because they show that Angels are still doing God's bidding on this planet and in our lives.

The State Trooper and The Lady in White happened to friends of mine. They were excited when they related their divine experiences, and I have no reason to doubt them.

The Alabama fan I first heard from a family member and then read it in the local newspaper. I do believe that God puts the right people in the right places at the right time to do the right thing.

My story is just that, it happened to me. Why? I have not led hundreds or thousands to the Lord. Maybe it happen because he loves me. Maybe it happened because you needed to read this story, or a particular chapter. I know God will go to extremes to help one person. He saved my life, maybe he will touch yours.

Chapter 13

Regaining your wow

Introduction:

The school child watches wide eyed while the egg begins to shake a little, then he notices a crack appear in the top of the shell, then a hole. A tine bird head pushes its way through the shell and only word that escapes the child's mouth is "WOW".

WOW:

To overwhelm with delight or amazement (World Book Dictionary)

Morning glories and wildflowers

Beautiful gifts form God

To busy to notice

Take time:

Hear the music of the wind

Artistry of sunsets

Stars on a calm lake

Glories in Heaven and on earth:

Isaiah 61:3

1st Chronicles 29:11

Psalms 96:6

> *Does it hurt God's feeling when we do not appreciate His gifts to us?*

How Great Thou Art story

God is still active

Life is full of abundance

Psalms 8:1-9

Learn to say WOW

Chapter 14

Resurrection of the Heart

Introduction:

Jesus told Mary that He was the resurrection and the life; of course, He was speaking of the resurrection of the dead but sometimes more things than the body dies. People have all kinds of things to die in their lives. Has your hope died, how about your love or faith? Has someone killed your spirit or ambition? Has your enthusiasm been smothered, your compassion stomped out? Does your attitude stink like it has died? There are a lot of things that we go through that can kill part of the soul. John 10:10 tells us that the thief comes to kill, steal and destroy. It is not just the body he is after but also the heart. He is constantly attacking the heart. He is the master of the heart attack.

Eight attributes:

Hope - Love - Faith - Spirit - Ambition - Enthusiasm - Compassion - Attitude

Mary Magdalene and lost hope:

John 20: 1-18

Jesus was everything to Mary

Mary's hope died with the death of Jesus

Went to the tomb

Heard her name

The legend of Mary and the egg

Elijah and lost faith:

Greatest of Prophets

1st Kings 19: 1-4

Jezebel's threat

Elijah's flight

Get alone with God

He is still with you

Gives Strength

Get out of comfort zone

Realize that you are not alone

The Samaritan woman and lost love:

John 4:4-26

Jesus had to go through Samaria

Not the road the Jews took

Jesus stepped out of tradition into taboo

Jesus stepped out of Heaven to the cross

Jesus filled her heart

Her heart overflowed to the city people

Jonah and the other five attributes:

Jonah's disposition - Jonah 4:1-11

Jonah lost:

His compassion for lost souls

His attitude of a Godly man

His ambition to work for God

His enthusiasm to preach

His spirit

God prepared:

A whale

A gourd

A worm

A vehement east wind and hot sun

God let Jonah see things from His perspective

Revelation 3:20 : Open the door of your heart wide

When you are troubled

The Prince of Peace will come in

When you are mourning

The Father of comfort will come in

When you are sick or hurting

The Healer will come in

When you are bound

The Deliverer will come in

When you are lost

The Savior will come in

Whatever your need

Jesus is the answer

Chapter 15

Mysteries and Secrets

Introduction:

There are some mysteries and secrets in the Bible that we need to learn that may build our relation with God.

The Mystery of the third Temple:

The first Temple

Built by Solomon

God moved in (1st Kings 8:10-11)

Destroyed by Nebuchadnezzar

The second Temple

Zerubbable and the people rebuild the Temple

Herod the Great remodeled the Temple

Romans destroyed the Temple in AD 70

The third Temple:

Temple built in Jerusalem in last days

Third temple is the body of Christ

John 2:19

1st Corinthians 3:16-17 we are the Temple

The Temple doors:

Talmud told of the doors opening by themselves

Josephus told of the doors opening by themselves

A.D. 30 year Christ died

God moved out of the man made Temple

Door of man - Revelation 3:2

God moves in when door is opened

The Secret place of the stairs:

Song of Solomon 2:4

Best of all songs

Relationship

Jesus and the Believer

Bridegroom and the Bride

Hebrew wedding

Engaged =married (Joseph was going to divorce Mary before the wedding)

Man leaves to build home

Trumpets blow upon his return

He takes her home

John 14:1-3

Step to access God's presence

First step - Delight - Psalms 34:4

Second step - Desire - Psalms 42: 1-2

Third step - Dependence on God

The Secret of God:

Job 29: 4

Secret=cowd=intimacy (by implication)

Tabernacle= ohel=dwelling place

Intimate with God at home

Live a life of Praise

Live a life of Gratitude

Chapter 16

Thanks a Lot

Introduction:

Gratitude = consist of being more aware of what you have, than what you do not. (Author Unknown)

The story of Queen Juliana of the Netherlands.

Gratitude:

A Lifestyle

Health benefits

Emotional benefits

Bible on Gratitude:

1st Thessalonians 5:18 (In all things)

Ephesians 5:20 (For all things)

Romans 9:28 (How can we do it)

Hebrews 13:15 (Even in hard times)

Count your Blessings

The Ten Lepers: Luke 17:11-19

Thankfulness important to Jesus

The nine in their excitement forgot

We forget to thank God for many of our blessings

> *Deuteronomy 26:11 And thou shalt rejoice in every good thing which the Lord thy God hath given unto thee, and unto thine house, thou, and the Levite, and the stranger that is among you.*
>
> *Psalms 92:1 It is a good thing to give thanks unto the Lord, and to sing praises unto thy name, O most High:*

Chapter 17

The God of Broken Pieces

Introduction:

The English Civil War took place between 1642 and 1651 and consisted of three different armed conflicts between the Parliamentarians, those that supported the Parliament, and the Royalist, those that supported the King. During the second conflict the town of Colchester, a walled city with a castle and several churches, was fortified by the Royalist and was laid siege by the Parliamentarians. Standing next to the city wall was St. Mary's Church, a huge cannon was placed on the wall of St. Mary's Church to defend the city. In mid July a shot from a Parliamentary cannon damaged the wall of St. Mary's Church that supported the cannon and the cannon went crashing to the ground. The cannon was so big that the Royalist soldiers and Calvary could not pick up the cannon and place it on another wall. Toward the end of August, with the lost of the cannon the Royalist had to lay down their arms, open the gates of Colchester and surrender. The cannon that defended the city of Colchester had a famous name, Humpty Dumpty. Humpty Dumpty did not become an egg until illustrated in Lewis Carroll's story "Through the Looking Glass".

Humpty Dumpty sat on a wall

Humpty Dumpty had a great fall

All the Kings horses and all the Kings men

Could not put Humpty Dumpty together again.

The King (Jesus):

Can put you back together

Broken pieces

Missing pieces

Fill in the voids

Ruth:

Ruth 1: 1-4

Bethlehem = house of bread

Famine in the house of bread

Find a place to be fed

The providers die

Ruth's perspective:

Forbidden foe Israelite to marry a Moabite

Forbidden for Moabite to enter temple

Ruth in the linage of Jesus

Moved with Naomi to Israel

God rescued and put their lives back together

Others in the Bible who lost their world:

Adam and Eve

Lost garden

Lost first two children

Noah

Lost all but immediate family

His whole world washed away

Inherited the whole world

Abraham

Left his home

Conflict between servants and nephew

Lot kidnapped

Blessing long time coming

Job

Lost business

Lost children

Lost wife

Lost friends

Lost hope

Encountered God

God put his life back together

How long does it take the hurting to stop?

May take years

God will be with you

God will give you little gifts along the way

God will help you see things that will help you heal

Give God the pieces

Chapter 18

Regaining Your Smile

Introduction:

> *O my soul, why be so gloomy and discouraged? Trust in God! I shall again praise him for his wondrous help; he will make me smile again, for he is my God!*
> *Psalms 43:5 (Living Bible)*

Someone once said that people smile at people who smile. Give it a try.

Studies on smiling:

Benefits for you and those around you

More oxygen to the brain

Makes you feel better

Sends out a positive message

Makes you look younger

Lowers blood pressure

Helps you relax

Boost your immune system

> *A smile costs nothing but gives much. It enriches those who receive without making poorer those who give. It takes but a moment, but the memory of it sometimes lasts forever. None is so rich or mighty that he cannot get along without it and none is so poor that he cannot be made rich by it. Yet a smile cannot be bought, begged, borrowed, or stolen, for it is something that is of no value to anyone until it is given away. Some people are too tired give you a smile. Give them yours, as none needs a smile so much he who has no more to give. (Author Unknown)*

Jacob and Esau:

Jacob cons Esau out of his birthright

Jacob steals Esau's blessing

Jacob runs for his life

Jacob is conned

Jacobs blessing is stolen

Jacob goes home

Jacob fears for his life

Esau smiles

A lot can be seen in a smile, a lot happens inside the person receiving a smile, and a lot happens inside the person giving a smile. So smile.

William Shakespeare said in *Othello,* "The robbed that smiles, steals something from the thief."

An Unknown Author said, "The shortest distance between two people is a smile."

Mother Teresa said, "Every time you smile at someone, it is an action of love, a gift to that person, a beautiful thing." So smile.

Chapter 19

Under the Influence

Introduction: Tell story of "Little Boy Lost"

It is no secret that we will become what we hang around. That is the reason the only people who want to hear you complain is people who has something to complain about, or on the more positive side people smile at people who smile. If something as simple as a smile can influence another person's attitude then we all should be smiling.

Psalms 42:1-4

Hart is a small deer

Submerse in water

Waters to swim in

Psalms 42:3

David could not feel God

God will never leave nor forsake

Things separate man from God

David's friends

We heard of your battle with the bear and lion God was with you then, where is He now?

We saw you kill the giant; God was with you then, where is He now?

We saw you dance before the ark; God was with you then, where is He now?

We saw you lead a kingdom with the guidance for God, Where is He now?

David was alone, and could not find God.

If your life were a book

Would it

Inspire

Discourage

People who influenced

J.R.R. Tolkin influenced C.S. Lewis

Andrew influenced Peter – John 1:40

Barnabas influenced Paul – Acts 9:27

Bad Influence

Alcohol and drugs

Friends and peers

Society

Television

Good Influence

Holy Spirit

Bible

Love

Jesus under the Influence

Holy Spirit

Luke 4:1

Luke 4: 18

Love held Jesus to the cross

How feel the influence of the Holy Spirit

Learn and meditate on the Word

Pray in silence

Step out

Chapter 20

Regaining your footing

Introduction:

Sometimes we are hit so hard by the circumstances of life it knocks us down and sometimes knocks the breath out of us, even when we are wearing the armor of God. Let us take a look at the armor and see if there is anything, we can do to help our armor from being pierced.

Ephesians 6:11-17:

Paul under house arrest in Rome

Knew about armor

God's protective resources

Belt of truth:

Gospels are truth

Jesus :

Born of a virgin

Lived sinless life

Died on a cross

Rose from the dead

Breastplate of righteousness:

Protects the heart

Righteousness=being made right

Gift from God

Feet shod with the preparation of the Gospel of Peace:

Live peaceably with all men

Jesus gives peace

Live in peace give no ammo to Satan

Shield of faith:

Shield covered the entire body

2nd Samuel 22:3

God is our shield

Hebrews 11:1

Believing without seeing

Helmet of Salvation:

Protection for the mind

Romans 12:2

Renew the mind

Learn to think on the positive things

Sword of the Spirit:

The sword is an offensive weapon

The enemy would have nothing to fear from us if we only had armor

Jesus defeated the devil with the word

Practice with the word

Psalms 119:11

There is nothing wrong in being hit by an assault of the devil, it happens to all of us. Sometimes we are hit so hard it knocks us down, we should never stay down but get back up and polish our armor, sharpen our swords and stand. When we have done all we can to keep standing, do not lose hope, it is at those times that God will hold us up. Never give up the fight. Remember you are not in this alone, you have brothers and sister in God that will help when you are tired that will guard when you need a breather, just do not stop, you will be needed to stand guard when someone else grows weary of the battle, do not let them down, you will need them someday.

Chapter 21

The Bethesda Syndrome

Introduction:

If you take a close look at the story of the pool of Bethesda, you may see our society, our Churches, and possibly sometimes ourselves.

John 3:5

Thirty eight years sick

Accepted state

Enjoyed pity

John 3:6

Do you want it

What do you prefer?

Handicap parking

Able to walk

I can do it attitude

John 3:7

Excuses

Lack of opportunities

Others take my opportunities

Symptoms of The Bethesda Syndrome

1. Hanging around a lot of negative influence

2. Sitting around doing nothing, waiting on a miracle from God.

3. Accepting your state (things will never change)

4. Blaming others for your condition

5. Not given opportunities

The cure

Get up

Do something

Chapter 22

The End

§

Introduction:

If you were to view a believer's life as a book, the funeral of that person would not be the end of the book but the conclusion of the first chapter. There is a lot more to come.

Chapter two of the believer's life:

II Corinthians 5:8

Absent from the body, present with Christ

Jesus is in heaven

The glories of heaven

Chapter three of the believer's life:

Believers called to heaven

Wedding banquet of the Lamb

Judgments on earth

Chapter four in the believer's life:

Battle where Satan is bound for a thousand years

Life on earth 1,000 plus first life

Life of peace

Chapter five in the believer's life

Season were Satan is let loose

Final defeat of Satan

Chapter six of the believer's life

Eternity

No the end

CPSIA information can be obtained
at www.ICGtesting.com
Printed in the USA
BVHW031515110620
581230BV00002B/61